Favourite Walks in Three Counties

Favourite Walks in Three Counties

Keith Taylor

Five Leaves

Favourite Walks in Three Counties
by Keith Taylor

Published in 2000 by Five Leaves Publications
PO Box 81, Nottingham NG5 4ER

Photographs: Keith Taylor unless specified.

Five Leaves gratefully acknowledge financial assistance
from East Midlands Arts

east midlands arts
making creative opportunities

Printed in in Great Britain
Deisgn by 4 Sheets Design & Print Limited

ISBN 0 907123 28 7

Contents

Index of Maps

Acknowledgments

No such guide book could be produced by one person alone and I wish first to thank Ross Bradshaw for his keen interest in the project.

Thanks also to my small but ever observant group of friends: Denis Astle; Andrew Bradley; Peter Dawson and Tony Stevenson. Each contributed, in some way, to the exploration of the particular paths we were walking and were always generous with their time, transport and companionship.

Along the way, National Trust wardens, equestrians, ramblers, water bailiffs, retired colliers, pub landlords and anglers also added items of local fact and legend. Though I failed to learn their names, each meeting proved valuable.

For the manuscript layout, maps and illustrations I am grateful to writer and artist Amanda Jayne Ward, for so admirably reproducing the maps, and to Margaret and Gordon Gadsby for making me aware of her talents.

When the walks were completed the text was handed to Alison Hastie, an expert when dealing with tight schedules, who not only deciphered my longhand, but was aware of the time factor throughout.

Preface

The idea for this book was conceived by the publisher, but the locations are those I have thought the most interesting of the maze of footpaths I have been exploring over the past twenty or thirty years.

Unlike many walking guides, this one crosses county boundaries and borders in my attempt to interpret the wildlife, industrial archaeology, and aspects of village and country estate life in parts of Leicestershire, Nottinghamshire and Derbyshire. Some of the routes are well-known; others less so. For walkers and their families living outside the region I have suggested the M1 motorway as a link and in the information panels given the appropriate junction between Loughborough and Chesterfield, from which each suggested parking place and route can be reached.

A number of routes are interlinked so that walkers have the choice of exploring between one and four tracts of countryside and therefore extending or reducing their mileage as they think best for the individual itinerary. By doing this, the out-of-region walker will not have driven a number of miles just to embark upon one relatively short walk.

In areas which attract wildlife I have also added a 'seasonal guide' so that time can be set aside for studying the behaviour patterns of the many bird and (admittedly fewer) mammal species that will hopefully appear.

I have not overlooked the fact that people also enjoy exploring country towns and have suggested several as bases from which these localised explorations could begin, particularly if you are interested in staying overnight.

The maps are taken from my own rough sketches, but beautifully enhanced by Amanda Jayne Ward. They are not to scale but have been produced as quick directional guides.

A Choice of Directions

Beginning in the Charnwood Forest country, the chosen walks vary from long established and conserved country estates to land tracts reclaimed after colliery waste exploitation where the land has in most cases been purchased by the serving council and fittingly landscaped to become a modern country park. Similarly, belts of ancient woodland and hedgerow compare with coverts that have been badly neglected but are being conserved today by stalwart bands of volunteers.

I have included the Nottingham urban fringe and the paths through and around the nearby section of the Trent Valley and its gravel extraction areas, the winding towpaths of the Erewash, Nottingham and Cromford canals and the woodland and field paths on the edge of the Derbyshire foothills.

I should add that while the rolling acres of Calke and Staunton Harold may prove pleasing to the eye some of the outcropping between Ironville and Pinxton will not. Further round that particular route, the paths alongside the fields and farms make up for what seems to have been lost.

One or two of the routes have become available due to the trust and foresight of private landowners residing in the Staunton Harold and Severn Trent Water Authority areas. They have allowed us 'permissive paths' across land tracts that were previously closed to the public. Such 'permission' can be withdrawn if it is decided that a route is being misused.

I have not included the Derbyshire Peak District because there are so many excellent guides already available for those intending to explore this region.

Time Out Around Charnwood Forest

The Leicestershire Highlands

Situated six miles from Leicester and with contours discernible from the M1, the hills and deeply wooded valleys of the Charnwood Forest Country have acquired the title 'Leicestershire Highlands' since the days of tourist brochure marketing.

These thirty square miles comprising private and publicly owned estates, hillside woodlands and glistening, picturesque streams and rivers are overlooked by the Beacon, Bardon and Warren Hills. The slate quarry tracts around Swithland reveal hidden grottos, grazing Highland cattle and several interesting reservoirs which tempt every motorist and cyclist to stop and have a look round no matter how tight the itinerary. For me, perhaps because of the colour and play of low sunlight across bracken slopes and sections of stone walling, Charnwood Forest is essentially autumn and winter country.

Charnwood? How did the name come about? The question was answered for me by a Field Officer employed at the New Walk Museum, Leicester. He explained that Charnwood was originally called Cernewoda; the 'cerne' having derived from 'carn' which in Welsh means rock.

The name must have originated from the thick and widely spread woods providing all the natural resources for the charcoal industry, from which the area became known.

The Lure of Place Names

In the summer of 1952, I persuaded my mother to give me the twenty-one shillings needed to buy a book displayed on the shelves of the old Sisson and Parkers bookshop in Nottingham.

The book's title was *This Wild Company,* and was written by the late John Stacey. It fired me with a continuing enthusiasm for exploration and the resolve to keep field notebooks of my own and buy a reputable camera to illustrate points of interest in the future.

John Stacey's book also gave me a penchant for place names. On waking at first light each Saturday morning with the prospect of a weekend's local wanderings ahead, I studied the Charnwood place names mentioned by the bird-watching author and noted that while some were self explanatory, others gave little or no clues to an environmental location.

High Tor, One Barrow, Blackbrook, Stoney Hollow, Warren Hills, Timberwood Planation, Agar Nook, High Sharpley, Charley Mill, Burrow Wood, Bardon... Where were they and how far? Could you cycle there and back in a day?

Later that summer my sister and her fiancé toured the Charnwood Forest Country by motorcycle and open-topped sportscar. They came home with tales of cream teas served in the cottage parlours of Swithland village and Woodhouse Eaves, streams rippling between ledges of green mossed rocks, willow branches reflected in the mirror of Groby Pool. They took me out to Beacon Hill one sweltering July afternoon and as we walked the steep incline, and the surrounding countryside opened up on either side, I told myself that this was a good place to be. I experienced a kinship with John Stacey who knew the country then as I know it today, and I continue seeking the charm and intrigue of this often overlooked high ridge of the once heavily industrialised English Midlands.

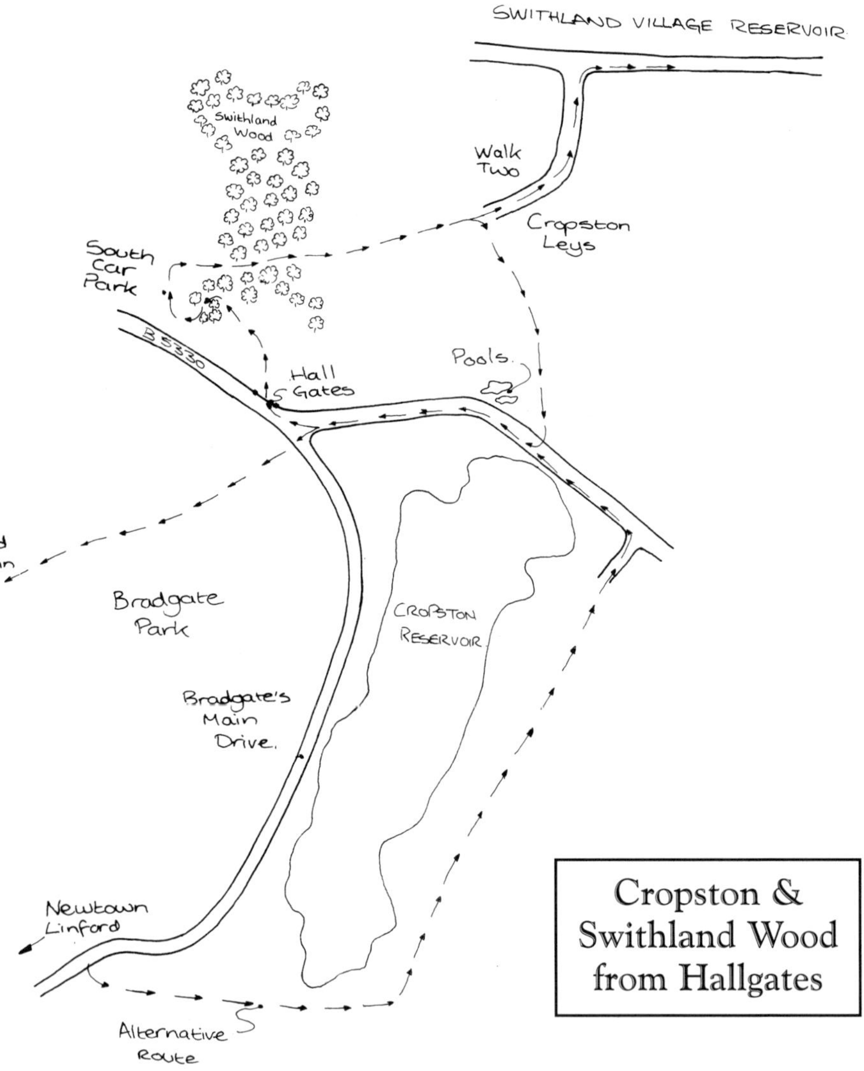

Cropston & Swithland Wood from Hallgates

Exploring Bradgate, Swithland Wood and Cropston

M1 Junction:	22 linking with A50 or 23 linking up with A512
Map Reference:	Pathfinder 874 SK4/51
Start:	Main car park by All Saints Church, Newtown Linford
Car Parking:	Entrance car park, Pay and Display
Buses:	From Derby Bus Station — A26 From Loughborough — as below from High Street From Leicester St. Margarets— 120, 123 Sundays 121 only Haymarket Bus Station (Stand C12) Midland Fox Busline 0116 2511411 for enquiries for all three bus stations
Refreshments:	The cafés near the park entrance The Bradgate or The Lin, Newtown Linford
Distance:	5½ miles approx.
Duration:	2–2½ hours depending on route chosen

Recommended Reference Guide

The best researched and most recent book embracing Bradgate's social and natural history, geology and local legends is usually on sale at one of the information outlets and at Newtown Linford's post office. The title is *Bradgate Park* by Joan Stevenson and Anthony Squires and is published by Kairos Press. The current price is £3.50, for an attractive and sensibly priced work which makes interesting reading whether you are exploring

Bradgate on foot or relaxing beside the fire.

About The Walks

Bradgate is a deer park, but with a difference due to the heathland, rock formations, drystone walls, plantations, uneven ridges and aged oaks which depict a quite dramatic and moody landscape. Swithland Wood, by contrast, is perhaps what one would expect with its clearings, tall oaks and bracken slopes. But the change recurs on the pleasing haul back through Bradgate to its highest point then down to Newton Linford; a picturesque village from which other parts of Charnwood can be explored. Sensible footwear is recommended.

The Route

Bradgate has many paths but so far as diversity of wildlife and landscape is concerned, I prefer the main drive leading directly through the park from Newtown Linford to Hallgates and Cropston.

On entering, the rocks and aged oaks dominate. Within yards you become aware of the jackdaws, woodpigeons and a few grey squirrels.

The fallow and red deer are free roaming but you are requested not to feed them. During the autumn the fallow deer in particular can be seen foraging for acorns or couched and cudding beneath the oaks.

These oaks are naturally bedded close to rock formations. The monkey puzzle trees, Cedar of Lebanon and high slopes provide rather a unique setting, at least so far as the average deerpark is concerned.

This area is called 'Little Matlock' but the wildlife potential hereabouts makes it more interesting than the Derbyshire mecca of Matlock itself.

Over to the right are the gentle staircased pools of the River Lyn. Moorhens skulk through the sedges and below the surface there are small trout, minnows and crayfish.

Where the drive meets with the bracken and a length of what appears to be dry ditch over on your left, pause to take in the walled sanctuaries of Elder Plantation, Bowling Green Spinney and Dale Spinney.

On the right some natural erosion beneath the oaks and close to the Lyn's winding course should tempt you to spend a few minutes with *Bradgate Park* and its references to the old park pale, medieval ditch and bank.

As you continue walking the ruins of Bradgate House begin to dominate while the slopes of the deer sanctuary (which is closed to the public) sweep down to the edge of a grass tract, beyond which is a stand of oaks and bracken, then a field with its boundary wall flanking Cropston Reservoir.

Deer enthusiasts refer to this as 'the deerfield' which is again closed to the public. The deer, however, can be studied here through binoculars.

Alternative Path

At the bridge over the Lyn, a path crosses directly to a gate in the wall on the opposite side. If there are deer grazing, pathside disturbance should be kept to a minimum. If in September, October or early November a stag is roaring and lording around a herd of hinds and followers, then still cross, but detour around the entire assembly and put at least forty feet between yourself and the deer.

One brisk sunlit morning I paused at a distance to view a stag and thirty or forty hinds and followers couched and cudding here. They were closely bunched and when a collie dog appeared from the bracken only one hind rose. To her, the dog represented a predator, as would a fox, and with tail held upright and body tensed she pursued the twisting and

Section of stone walling: Swithland

turning dog across the entire width of field just as if it been June, when she would probably have had a dappled calf curled and hidden in the bracken.

When you reach the gates in the wall, turn left and follow the footpath with Cropston Reservoir over to your left. Usually a plank bridge leads you over the ditch and by the field boundary wall footpath extending the length of the reservoir.

On my latest walk along this path, kale was the productive crop and pheasants broke from it or skulked beneath the overhangs of broad leaf. At dusk, lapwings can be seen going to roost in kale although many join the waders on and around the inflow gravel spits around reservoirs.

Where this path ends and you have reached the main road, bear left and follow the reservoir-head wall back to Cropston and the Hallgates car park.

The Original Walk continued

On the slopes around the oaks you may well encounter the free-ranging peafowl, and by one of the fenced oaks a notice informs you that Queen Adelaide, aunt of Queen Victoria and wife of William IV, took her ease beneath the tree during her visit in July 1842.

The tract of land between the ruins and Deer Park Spinney occasionally attracts a green woodpecker to sift through the mole heaps or ants' nests, but you need to be glassing through your 'scope' or binoculars when the bracken is low, and not always from the main drive.

The toilet block and Visitor Centre are situated close to the reservoir wall over to your right, while opposite, the Keeper's House appears imposing against the background of trees.

Twenty or so years ago this end of Cropston Reservoir was relatively windswept, but today a wide variety of willows with, I suspect, some alder, have been planted around the margins and serve as adequate windbreaks as well as habitat for small birds like titmice and siskins.

If you are a bird watcher and frustrated by the height of the reservoir wall then make your way across, because viewing slots allow you to scan the spits and inflow region where waders occasionally feed, and in the autumn and winter, the reservoir attracts a variety of gulls in to roost.

My son and I saw our first inland cormorants following the Lyn down to Cropston, but my most memorable experience occurred on an October morning when fog began unexpectedly screening the hills and ridges of the parkland. Close to the Visitors Centre a darkly wallowed stag paraded around a group of hinds but beyond them the trees had become obscured.

The reservoir by comparison was free of fog for a time, and when we turned from these viewing slots a mixed 'wisp' of snipe and green sandpipers almost collided with us. One green sandpiper was so close I could have grabbed it. Its dark rounded eye, white, lightly mottled crop and black barred wingtips were distinctive as it prepared to settle, disorientated no doubt by the blanketing fog.

As most birdwatchers will know, green sandpipers, although migratory, winter on our south coast in small numbers. Those on this collision course must still have been on passage.

Back to the main drive, our walk continues with the undulating ledges of grass, bracken and rock on your left, although paths lead up and over the parklands. The Hallgates car park, with Swithland Wood beyond, is to be found in a few hundred yards where the reservoir wall turns.

Walk Two is now described but if you wish to return to Newtown Linford, the continuation of Walk One will be found on page 13.

Walk Two/Hallgates — Swithland Woods

Distance: 2¾ miles

Duration: Approx 1 hour

Leave Bradgate by the Hallgates car park. Bear left and cross the B5330 noticing the splendid white house, Hallgates, and gravel drive with the magnificent Wellingtonia pine towering alongside.

You should be facing oncoming traffic with Horseshoe Cottage Farm on your right. In the autumn the ploughed field on the opposite side of the road contrasts with the green of the woodland covert overlooking higher ground.

Yellow-hammers flock here in the autumn and winter, often with meadow-pipits and skylarks among them.

When you reach the fence and signpost for Swithland, climb the stile and follow the well-used path across the old pasture field.

Goldfinches can be seen feeding on the thistle heads, and red admiral, peacock and small tortoiseshell butterflies also enhance the summer scene.

Over to your left is a stand of trees, the majority of them crab apple and hazel with, lower down the row, a fine oak or two. Look for the jays which feed here in the autumn, sometimes four to six at a time and take in, through binoculars, their conspicuous colours as they fly, calling harshly, towards Swithland Wood over to your right.

The path narrows to the post-and-rail fence, alongside which the brook splashes. Cross the bridge and climb the stile, then look again at the bridge and the way in which it has been constructed, using what appears to be old ceiling beams joined together. They are more likely to have come from a cottage than a barn.

In the wood a choice of directions; the north or south car park; but for this walk you need to turn left and follow the woodland and field boundary fence and hedge around to the left, where, after you have turned the corner, a stand of holly suggests that it was definitely planted with field boundary indication in mind.

The sonorous cooing of wood-pigeons fills the wood on summer days and in the autumn you will see the birds foraging for acorns, both in the oak branches and on the ground. Turn right into the south car park and on the right, as the nearby pumping stations outlet unit comes into sight, turn right along the ridge road.

Swithland's varied oaks are surprisingly tall. You will no doubt also identify ash, lime and rowan saplings, mature silver birch and sycamore here.

The bridle road skirts the post-and-rail boundary fence to your right and the track, stoney and uneven, rises to well above fence level. There are many fox and badger trails.

Eventually the field corner gives way to woodland on both sides and the bracken slopes and tall oaks dominate.

You will hear greater and lesser spotted woodpecker and nuthatch throughout the spring and you may well glimpse the occasional tree creeper.

At the next junction, turn right and continue between the oaks to the field-end junction then climb a stile taking you out of the wood alongside a narrowly fenced path, the land contours gently rising by Swithland

Wood over on your left. The path continues along to Cropsten Leys and the Swithland Walk but if you wish to return to Hallgates and Bradgate, take the footpath on the right.

This is a bullfinch hedgerow, although of course you will see other small birds. Notice the fox trails in the hedgebottom. I wonder how many foxes to the acre there are in Leicestershire?

The path continues across a field being currently grazed by two horses, as the sheds indicate. There may be some electrified wire positioned close by, so do take care.

The next stile takes you into a grassy field where signs indicate that people have strayed away from the path, because of the proximity of water.

The two ponds nurture various aquatic weeds below and water plants above. The tight willows will attract the occasional kingfishers, providing there are enough minnows and sticklebacks to feed them. You will hear moorhens calling as the adults seek out their chicks.

The occasional brace of mallard will be wild birds. Teal, snipe and redshank also explore the shallows of pools like this.

Continuing by the hedge you should see various finches and titmice. Then the path merges into a pleasant green lane with rowan, ash, haw and blackhorn thicketing either side.

Beyond the tubular gate is a road, so be ready for it! Having climbed the gateside stile, turn right and on to Bradgate Road.

The road forks, so take care. Face the oncoming traffic and use as your guide the sign *'Cropston ½ mile'*.

You need to be on Lodge Lane, which will take you up to the road skirting Cropston Reservoir.

Here you may see heron and cormorant. Keep the reservoir and its environs to your left and follow the wall by Bradgate Lodge, noticing the contours of Bradgate Park emerging boldly as the Hallgates car park comes into sight.

Walk One continued
Hallgates — Bradgate — Newtown Linford

Returning to Bradgate, if you want to stray from the main drive, bear right towards and beyond the picnic tables, and take the path by the walled wood on your left known as Coppice Plantation.

This path winds steadily uphill through the bracken and runnels and over and around several freshwater springs and pools. There is a choice of directions about every three or four hundred yards but usually I make for the highest point, since the walk in itself is food for the heart and lungs.

On the sides of every path or track you will see rabbit and fox droppings. Notice the closely planted pines and silver birches of the wood over on your right. The wood bears the interesting name of Sliding Stone Enclosure. If you are familiar with bird calls, you will most likely recognise the goldcrest and coal-tit which are attracted to pine and birch habitats, but from March to late May the laughing calls of the green woodpecker or 'yaffle' resound across the hills as breeding pairs of these birds explore for nesting sites the spinneys situated beyond the house ruins or close to the Keepers Lodge.

On windy days in the late summer or early autumn you may well see sizeable flocks of swallows and house martins hawking low over the bracken for winged insects which are also low due to the velocity of the wind.

When you have reached the high point on the horizon then continue over the tracks and up the green long slope to the highest point in the park, conspicuous by the turreted tower known as Old John, and the stable ruins described in *Bradgate Park*.

The descent can be made along any of the paths leading down from Old John and the 'toposcope' donated by the Newtown Linford villagers in 1953.

The path through Old John Spinney is interesting because this spinney is walled. One can imagine past gamekeepers rearing pheasant chicks for the autumn shoots here.

As the land contours rise and lower, so do the old hollowed oaks, outcrops of agglomerate rock and drystone walls.

On this long descent keep an eye open for summer visitors like the redstart. Some years ago a little owl used to hunt in the noonday heat around this terrain, although its youngsters were probably huddled in a nest hole situated beyond the boundary walls.

Looking Around Newtown Linford

Marion's Cottage, at the Newtown Linford car park, serves as an interpretive centre, but at the time of going to press is closed on Mondays and

Tuesdays.

The village church, All Saints, welcomes everyone to its Sunday 8 and 11.00 am services. For those seeking refreshment there are neighbouring cafés on the opposite side of the road, between the post office and garden centre.

Newtown Linford's thatched cottages are all individual in style. Some have small walled gardens close to the road while others are surrounded wholly or partially by garden shrubs and trees. Even the bus stop provides something of interest; pied wagtails flitting over from the stream and the robins seeking food for their chicks.

The Groby Footpath and Pool

Situated 1½ miles from Bradgate is an attractive thirty-four acre roadside lake. Its car park is now positioned within the second turning on the right, after you have driven by with the stretch of water again on your right.

When I first visited Groby Pool in the early 1960s you could pull the car in over the grass and scan the water surface through binoculars. A decade later the scene had changed entirely, the grass almost non-existent and feral ducks and geese clamouring around the partially-submerged rocks for food.

The pool is privately owned and is a quite sizeable stretch of water. Over towards Pool House is an island and fine reed bed, although, like the Cropston and Swithland Reservoirs, the surface can become noticeably windswept.

There are at least two signposted footpaths linking Newtown Linford and Groby, but if you choose to visit by car you need to take the second turn on the left after leaving the Bradgate car park.

The pool is well-hidden, and on the winding descent first time visitors may think they have taken the wrong road. However the willows beyond the arable fields to your right will eventually indicate its whereabouts.

Notice how the road is much lower than the pool.

Once this road was busy with quarry lorries, transporting Groby stone for road strengthening and foundation layering, as well as wall construction.

Dowry Furlong Car Park

At the car park a notice informs you that the nearby two-acre nature reserve of Dowry Furlong has been leased by the Groby Parish Council.

Signs of medieval farming are clear in this landscape at certain times of the year. Reference is also made to Groby Quarry and the mineral railway used for transporting granite.

As you walk the fence and hedge path connecting the car park to Groby Pool notice the fox scats littering the hardcore surface and in the autumn the hip, haw and blackthorn or 'sloe' berries entangling the fence and wall sides.

When you leave the car park a turn right will take you to Groby and the nearby M1 motorway. A left turn will, of course, guide you back to Newtown Linford and the steep slopes of Bradgate Park. In many ways these resemble tracts of Exmoor as you view them on the Groby route descent.

Around Swithland Reservoir

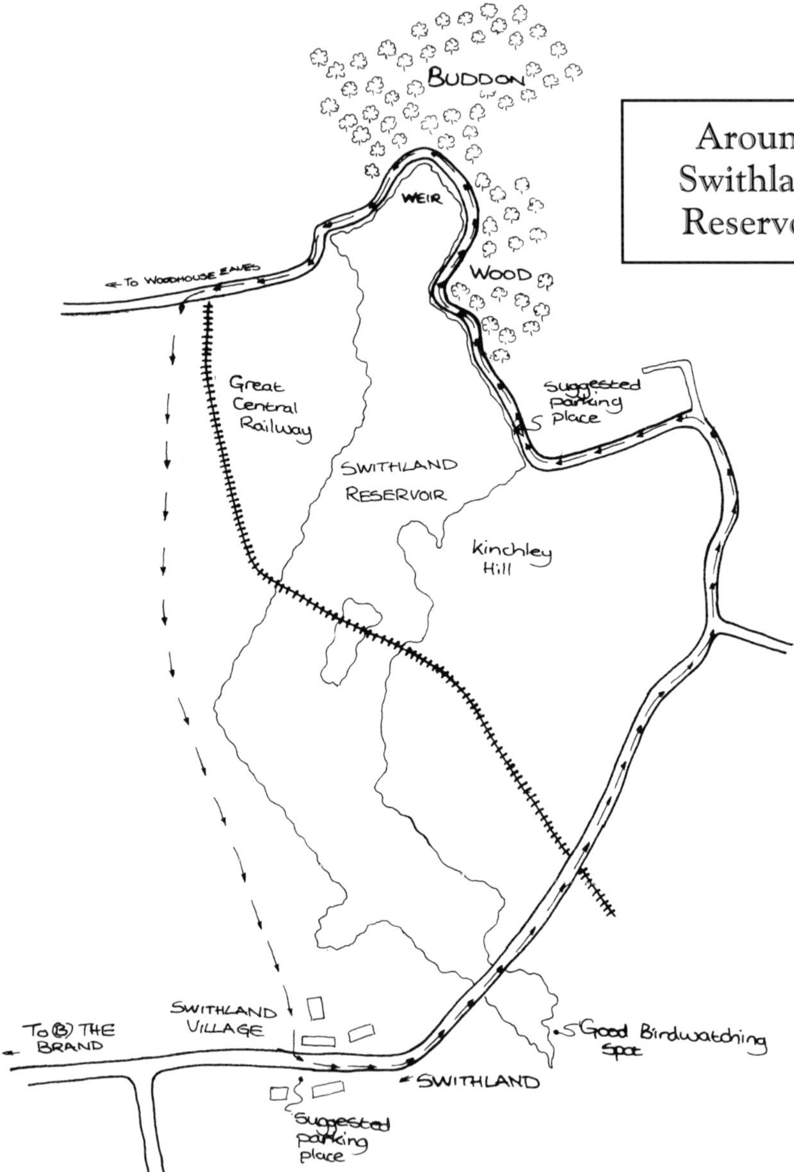

Swithland Village and Reservoir

M1 Junction:	22 linking with A50 or 23 linking up with A512
Map Reference:	Pathfinder 874 SK 41/5
Start:	Swithland Wood north car park situated between Swithland Village and Woodhouse Eaves
Buses:	123 Leicester Haymarket Bus Station From Loughborough High Street (stand C12) with Derby connections. Check with local Midland Fox offices (0116) 2511411
Refreshments:	The Griffin, Swithland Village
Duration:	2–2½ hours or longer if you are stopping at points of interest
Distance:	Approx 4½ miles.

About the Walk

As soon as you leave the car park, the individuality of the Charnwood Forest country meets you. The roots of oak and beech trees appear to be embedded in rock or sections of dry-stone walling. The quarry pools are situated on private land and have no admittance.

The first stretch of road recalls the age of slate quarrying. The quarries from which the Swithland slate and stone was extracted provided the walls, farmsteads and cottages from natural and local resources. We would be right to think of charcoal and slate on the walk between the car park and the village.

More than two-thirds of this walk takes you along a main and minor road, and progresses down to the side road skirting Swithland Reservoir's east bank.

Here there are contrasts between water and woodland, with Buddon Wood over to your right.

The side road takes you round by the waterworks plant at the north end of the reservoir then over the Great Central Railway bridge to a fieldgate and footpath sign on the left.

This section crosses fields grazed by livestock, particularly, in my experience, horses and ponies, so if you have a dog with you it needs to be leashed. In midsummer, providing it is dry, the distance can be covered in lightweight shoes. At other times it is advisable to wear boots, because the field paths are often muddy.

The Route

When you leave the car park you need to turn right and face oncoming traffic. Yet, perversely, three interesting aspects of the Charnwood Forest scene can be visited in line and are on the opposite side of the road. They can, however, be passed on the way back, because then you will again be facing oncoming traffic.

Assuming that you intend to spend a few minutes here at the beginning of your walk then just across the road to the left of the car park entrance are two relatively sheltered fields, in which twenty or so Highland cattle are occasionally grazed.

They vary in colour: buff, dark red and black, long-coated and wide horned, and make an impressive photographic study against the background woods.

In the winter they spend time beside the hay byre, full-fed no doubt and cudding, but at other times they feed along the roadside hedge and then it is possible to gain a photograph or two.

To the right of the cattle is a walled wood, private land I should stress, and a quarry.

It is possible from the roadside to study the quarry face when the leaves are off the trees in the late autumn and winter. Notice the stand of reeds way down in the quarry hollow. From there carry on along and almost down to the corner. Here is another flooded quarry overlooked by a tower built of local stone. Separating you from this dangerous site is a fine example of drystone walling.

Close to the wall stands a fine beech. Its trunk is again worth a photograph.

Down near the road corner, the green-lichened tree roots seem almost to have cut down through deeply embedded rock and if you do turn the corner you will see and hear the brook.

You need, however, to cross the T-junction here and bear right, so your back should be to the brook and the walled quarry. There is a pavement.

I find this a friendly walk. You will probably meet other walkers returning as well as horse and pony riders. Walking with friends one New Year's Day we were hailed by residents leaving their house, the midday lunch steaming on a plate in their hands, as they went to a neighbour's for the continuing celebrations.

Notice the individuality of the houses and cottages, the stonewalling and slate tiles. Some cottages have comparatively new chimneys while others still retain that look of a cosy homestead, probably with less physical hardship attached to cottage living than in times gone by.

Eventually the brook surges up to the roadside and serves as a double boundary to the relatively modern properties set back within the trees and beyond the lawns.

Each bridge spanning the brook is different from its neighbour. Look out for the island pool. Glimpse the moorhens grass-cropping alongside.

Opposite the splendid white cottage with the darkly-thatched roof is a gated small park. In the top right-hand corner stands a pillory. I could not determine whether it is a village relic or reconstruction. Nearby is a memorial seat dating from the mid 1950s. How long would such a seat exist if it were placed beside a pavement in one of our large industrial cities? On the right-hand side of the road stands The Griffin; another popular and welcoming hostelry, with a sizeable car park.

Across the road, a tower invites investigation. Similar towers are to be seen rising from the peripheral sections of farm wall farther round the village end.

Historians tend to disagree as to why such towers were constructed. I think they were probably granary towers.

The old name for 'granary', incidentally, was 'grange', which is why we frequently come across the name Grange Farm, particularly common in my native Nottinghamshire.

Swithland Hall is to the right as the road turns directly and the waterworks of the reservoir and the private buildings merge into the fields on the right. Look for lapwings here.

As the reservoir comes into sight, notice the gulls and coot among the wildfowl thronging the grass banks. These birds are interesting members of the rail family and have lobbed webbing along the side of each extended toe, unlike ducks and geese. In recent years a length of low barrier fencing has been extended along the railings, because coot and moorhens used to come out onto the road and pavement to be fed. The backwater is truly a waterbird paradise; its corners thick with reed, sedge, willow and alder thicket. The railway embankment keeps out at least some of the north-easterly wind.

Continue the walk by passing beneath the railway bridge. If it is a weekday you may flush a pheasant or two from the hedgerow and glimpse a hare or fox crossing the road.

Notice the fine oaks in the fields to the left and along the hedgerow to the right.

The pylons, though, prove a hazard to waterfowl and remind me of the occasion a colleague found two little grebe or dabchick, dead but still warm, beneath such wires at first light when this point highlights that waterfowl fly at night.

You should be still facing the oncoming traffic here and using the grass verge where possible. A number of oaks have ivy on the trunks to which butterflies and moths will be attracted. Birds will feed on the berries during the colder months.

As you approach the T-junction, notice the farm to the left and the village green type corner on the right. You need here to bear left by crossing the road carefully, by the signpost informing you that Mountsorrel is 1½ miles away.

You are now on Swithland Lane. There is a pavement on the right, so cross again, and continue by all the fine individual properties and across the top of Gypsy Lane.

Again the pylons are all too prevalent on the left, but eventually fields merge into the scene on either side. On the road bend, you begin a barely noticeable ascent and continue by a house with a splendid old oak gracing the front garden, with a traditional nestbox affixed to the oak's side. Now cross the top of Hampstead Road and notice the sign for Quorn. Continue by the tract of fields, the pylons and flanking willow wood then, not far from where the pavement peters out, there is a left turn into Kinchley Lane.

Kinchley is a noticeable descent (or ascent, depending on which direction you are taking). Kinchley Hill is worth glassing with the binoculars

A mute swan pen leads her newly hatched cygnets along the margins of Swithland Reservoir.

for meadow-pipits, yellow-hammers and skylarks; all of which form flocks throughout the autumn and winter.

Eventually the reservoir can be seen again. The road is interesting because it allows for contrasting views across the open water with the bracken, larch and silver birch sequences of Buddon Wood on your right.

Notice the rock formations here. On a morning in May with the haze of young foliage around you, blackbirds singing and woodpeckers drumming, a feeling of well-being settles over you — and with good reason!

Buddon Wood is on the eastern side of the reservoir. You cover its width by turning with the road, so that eventually Buddon is at your back and the private grounds of the waterworks buildings on your right.

This end is popular with birdwatchers as grebes and divers can be seen submerging quite close to the wall, beside which the modern 'scopes' are offered an uninterrupted view across the expanse of water.

By the private house, the road turns. Go with it. The wooded tracts on either side attract all the expected finches and titmice, the three species of woodpecker and summer visiting warblers; the same birds that you would expect to see and hear in Buddon Wood.

There is another good viewing point where the road bends to the right. This again is a corner favoured by the waterfowl, grebe and gull enthusiasts.

The bridge ahead takes you across the Great Central Railway line. If the trees are bereft of foliage on the embankments to your left, you will see the nest holes hewn into the trunks by woodpeckers.

To the right, at the time of writing, there is a sizeable rabbit warren and further along, you may pick out a fox earth used spasmodically by a breeding vixen.

Continue between the hedgerows until you see a footpath sign to your left, then ease through the gate and over the fields and stiles.

This route will eventually take you to the Swithland road and here you need to turn right. What happens if you continue along the lane and between the hedgerows? You will arrive at the delightful village of Woodhouse Eaves but you then need to swing left in order to join up with the winding and undulating road that takes you back to Swithland village.

Seasonal Highlights

The Spring Walk

Terns are common and the arctic, black and common can occasionally be seen. Common sandpipers, redshank and little ringed plover are also possibilities, while you can expect to see the yellow and pied wagtails and reed-buntings.

Birdwatchers familiar with the willow and marsh titmice may locate both here and great crested grebes are usually around in good numbers.

On such a sizeable stretch of water, the little grebe is more often heard than seen, but pairs frequent the backwater pools, as do ruddy ducks. Female ruddy ducks, when they submerge, take the entire brood of newly hatched ducklings with them. Pochard and kingfisher may also be glimpsed around the reeded edges, and greater and lesser spotted woodpeckers may be heard drumming from Buddon Wood, especially in the early morning.

The Summer Walk

Both the sparrowhawk and hobby have been recorded and green sandpipers, greenshank and dunlin may visit briefly.

The Autumn Walk

Black-necked grebe are not unknown here and by mid-October, goldeneye can be seen feeding close to pochard and tufted duck. Water-rails lure the birdwatchers to various backwater points and, on the surrounding fields, redwing and fieldfares feed while redpoll and brambling search through the seed and beechmast litter, and siskin visit the waterside alders.

The Winter Walk

Gull enthusiasts gather an hour or so before dusk to list the yellow legged, little and mediterranean gulls. One of the locally roosting peregrines may appear at the same time to take its last victim for the day.

Sea riding duck like smew and scoter, scaup and eider have flown in, and local birdwatchers occasionally record red-throated diver and rednecked grebe.

Adverse weather conditions greatly affect the movements of birds, and I well recall a February afternoon when freezing fog screened the entire reservoir. The silence was broken by the continual whistling of wigeon, then the repetitive hooting of four or five male tawny owls, disorientated by the fading light.

Swithland Slate

Between Quorn and Rothley, drywalling, similar to that in the Lake District, is common as you follow the dip and rise of the land..

The roofs of the cottages and farm buildings are laid with Swithland slate. Slate has also been shaped and used as gravestones hereabouts because of its durability. The Romans were the first to capitalise on this natural wealth and quarry the slate.

The diamond shaping of a slate was considered the vogue. Slate carving as a form of commercial art evolved from this, Hind and Polland later being considered master slate craftsmen.

As with almost every form of naturally acquired fibre, however, Swithland slate began to lose its popularity when Welsh slate became transportable and was deemed the best for roofing.

Swithland slate is greyish-green in colour, although there are variations. Slate that is noticeably green is recognised as having been quarried at Groby, whereas purple-russet or red-toned slate which enhances the cottages in Old Woodhouse was extracted from the place now known as Hanging Stone Rocks.

Red clay once provided an income for the founders and employees of Tuckers Brickworks which closed its gates in 1965. Closer to the Leicester boundary, near Syston, William Davis's gravel and sand extraction plant has altered the landscape, providing flooded pits that are now used for surfing, yachting and wildlife conservation and known locally as Wanlip Gravels.

Exploring the Derbyshire/Leicestershire Border

About the walks:
These three walks can be included as one by beginning at Melbourne, walking the short distance to Staunton Harold Reservoir and embarking on **Walk Two** which guides you alongside this stretch of water and over the ridged fields to the parklands of Calke Abbey. **Walk Three** connects Staunton Harold Hall by way of the permissive paths which round on to the main centre before you return through Calke and retrace your steps beside the reservoir to Melbourne.

Melbourne Pool

A good way for a small group to do this is to have one car parked at Calke or Staunton Harold, then drive back to Melbourne in the second car and begin from there. The entire duration for all three walks is about four and a half hours; the distance about eight and a half miles.

M1 Junction: 23A linking up with A453

Walk one: Melbourne Pool

Car Parking: Limited parking by the Melbourne Hall estate yards

Buses: From Nottingham – Runway 5 via E. Midlands Airport.
Phone Nottingham City Transport 950 3665
From Derby Bus Station – C68, C69 "Arriva Buses"

Distance: Approx 1 mile.

Duration: Allow 1 hour if birdwatching

The Route

This is best regarded as a birdwatching walk because you have to return the way you came, although Melbourne Hall grounds and gardens can be included in the exploration.

The walk begins at the entrance gates to Melbourne Hall, with the ornamental gardens to your left, and the pool to your right. Follow the drive down beside the water while trying to imagine how this tranquil scene would appear to the hall's residents past and present. Continue down by Pool House then, when the pool's outflow almost levels with the pool to your right, go through the handgate so that the fields are to your left. The woodland paths ahead are currently open to the public and you have a choice of sylvan and sequestered routes.

Where the woodland tract ends, you may well have to retrace your steps because this was, I understand, a concessionary path which, on my last visit, the owner had closed, allegedly due to the lack of public consideration. However, if there is a footpath sign, changes may have occurred. Assuming the path is closed (and the fence should indicate whether or not this is so), then you will have to return the way you came although there are two paths to explore — one beside the water and one through the woodland. When the concessionary path was open, the walker was allowed to cross the lake by the channel inflow, progress between grazing Friesian cattle and walk up two hilly fields to the village street and the circuit's completion.

The Seasonal Walks

The Spring Walk

Probably the first birds you will glimpse will be robin, wren and dunnock. Stroll down towards Pool House, pausing occasionally to glass the water. Most of the coot pairs are tolerant of human proximity. Watch them feeding among the surface weeds or submerging and 'up-ending', especially in May when they are searching for aquatic food with which to feed their chicks. The pool is divided into fifteen or so coot territories, with the subordinate pairs nesting among the submerged branches at the water's edge, their dominant neighbours occupying prime sites around the edges of those splendidly situated islands. The mallard, shovelers, ruddy duck and mute swan pair will dabble on the surface weed and 'up-end' but the swans will also submerge their necks and pull weed strands from the lake bed.

Incidentally, in March and April you may only see one swan for the mate will most likely be incubating on the island nest. The female or 'pen' will feed continually while she is egg-laying. Although one egg is laid every other day she will not begin the thirty-five day period of incubation until the full clutch has been laid. The male, or 'cob', therefore spends much time around the nest and eggs until the pen finally takes over. After the incubation period the cygnets begin to pip the shell and are escorted to the water a day or so later.

Moorhens are more wary at Melbourne than the coots. The garden banks adjacent to Pool House provide them with adequate nesting, perching and preening places.

Birds frequenting the walled garden to your left will bridge the two comparable habitats here. You may glimpse migrants such as the spotted flycatcher along with greenfinches, goldfinches, bullfinches, the inevitable blackbirds, blue, and great and long-tailed tits, all no doubt intent on finding food for their broods.

Follow the path round to the outflow gate, then cross the drive to scan the stream for kingfishers. Pied wagtails usually breed around here and you may see other small bird species coming down to drink. Having gone through the handgate by the outflow you could, in February, expect to hear a mistle thrush fluting from one of the nearby trees. Depending on the time of day, the field could also yield pheasant, partridge, snipe, lapwing, redshank, meadow-pipit, tree-pipit and skylark.

Glass the water again, if you haven't already, and study the courtship ceremonies of the great crested grebe: and the skittering or 'cat' behaviour mode, head turnings and ruff displays, the weed presentation ceremony. Little grebe pairs will also be nesting, usually around the island edges and lily pools. Ruddy duck drakes will usually be out there along with tufted and mallard. Mallard nest early and so, by mid-April, you could see the first broods of ducklings. Over by the island and church rear meadows bank, you will probably locate three or four herons preening and powdering their plumage.

The mixed wood provides habitat for all the expected woodland bird species, including the sparrowhawk and such summer migrants as the wood warbler and redstart. At least one breeding pair of tawny owls is resident, and goldcrests can be heard more often than seen, among the pines.

The Summer Walk

More or less the same as the Spring Walk, but with swallows and house-martins hawking for insects over the water. Spotted flycatchers — often regarded as 'sparrows' — are fairly prominent around the outbuildings and ornamental gardens.

The Autumn Walk

Mallard and other dabbling duck species begin pairing. Still scan the outflow stream for kingfisher but expect a grey wagtail or two along here. Out on the open water you may see tufted duck, gadwall, shoveler and ruddy duck. Throughout the season, pochard and wigeon will visit daily. You can often hear long-tailed fieldmice if you are quietly walking the woodpath.

The Winter Walk

All the usual garden and woodland birds will be foraging hard for food. The fields beyond the handgate attract flocks of fieldfare, redwing and small 'wisps' of snipe. In the woods the pungent scent of fox lingers around the prominent logs and tree trunks where each passing male has left his scent, for this is the mating or 'clikketing' season. Cygnets which have not left the swan pair indulge in daybreak circular flights around the area. If they have not left by the beginning of February they will be driven off by the adult pair . Coots begin sparring and exercising territorial rights. Woodcock can occasionally be flushed from the wood's edge and damp pasture near the inflow. Scan the tree-line for finches, titmice, woodpeckers, nuthatch and treecreeper.

Melbourne Hall — general information

Melbourne Hall is open to visitors in August only, but not on the first three Mondays of that month. The hours are 2.00-5.00pm.

The gardens are open from April to September 2.00-6.00pm on Wednesday, Saturday, Sunday and each bank holiday Monday.

Coach party organisers need to contact the curator — phone 01332-862502.

A brief history of Melbourne Hall and village will be on sale at the small, but efficient, interpretive centre.

The outbuildings

Up by the car park the estate's old workyards are worth a visit, for many of the smaller buildings have been renovated and are now used as craft workshops. Think how busy these inner yards would have been as they re-echoed with the grindings of the woodsaw and the voices of woodsmen, blacksmiths, brewers, bakers, laundry and dairy maids. The kennels housing the hound or beagle pack were situated close by.

Pub and refreshment note

On leaving the Melbourne Hall car park, turn left along Church Street and left again at the Buttercross. You are now on High Street which, as it bends, becomes Ashby Road. You are looking for the pub called the Melbourne Arms, on the right. If you intend to walk the Staunton Harold Reservoir to Calke route then continue by Robinsons Lane and, about a few hundred yards along on your right is the reservoir main entrance and car park and the beginning of **Walk Two**.

For the motorist

If you are exploring by car and seeking to enter Calke Park by the formal entrance, then turn right and follow Robinson's Hill to the bottom, turn left and continue down into Melbourne Lane and Main Street in Ticknall Village. When you see the Ticknall archway, turn sharp left over the cattle grid of Calke's formal entrance with the undulating parklands either side and the imposing avenue, originally of eighty-four lime trees, ahead.

Routes Around Calke & Staunton Harold

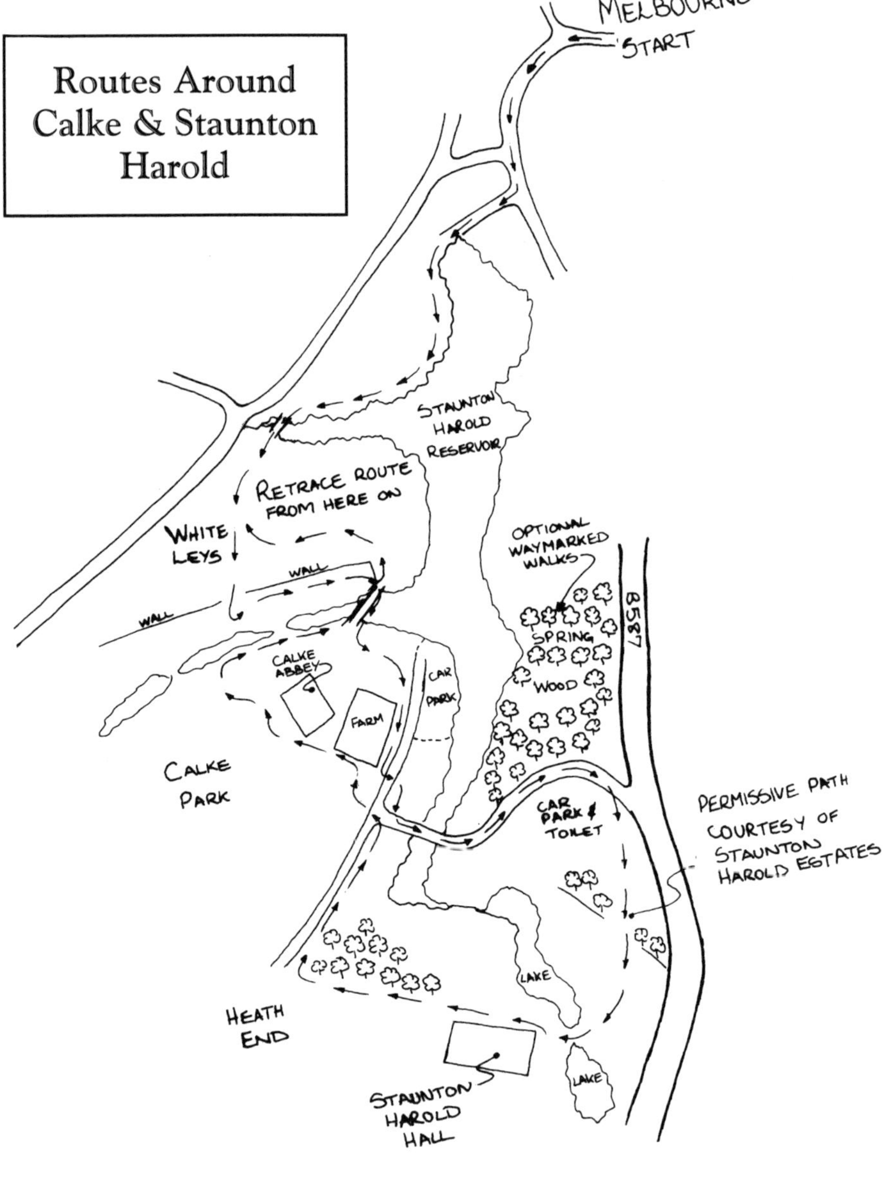

Walk Two: Staunton Harold Reservoir to Calke

Duration: 2½ hours (approx 1¼ hours each way)

Boots are recommended for winter walking.

The Route

The formal entrance to Staunton Harold Reservoir is bordered by the houses to the right, as you take the first turn after Robinson's Lane. Progress up the slope and, within yards, you will be looking down at the reservoir with its car parks, telephone kiosk, picnic and children's play area, situated alongside the toilets, interpretive centre and refreshment kiosk with outside seating.

Leave the car park and take the hardcore path extending alongside the scant plantations and sailing club premises. The signs interpreting the wildflower meadows are worth studying and, as you continue walking, you may see some thirty or so yachts out on the water, and more beached on the grass of the sailing club compound. Eventually the path curves and follows a long arm of the reservoir. In the autumn and winter the grass on both sides of the path is heavily grazed by wigeon on migration from the north.

This two hundred and nine-acre reservoir holds in the region of 1.4 billion gallons of water destined for the taps in and around the city of Leicester and most of the surrounding shires. It is fed partially by the streams threading in from the fields and pumping up the continual output yielded by the River Dove. There are always a few coot pairs feeding along the bank here. If you are walking in April look for the cowslips studding the grass stretch on your right.

Where the paths divide, turn right and uphill as the 'footpath' sign indicates, even though you will be tempted to take the narrow lane to the left to be near the water. On this higher road, known as Broadstone Lane, you will pass fields and private residences, each highly individual in style and character.

What you are looking for now is a tubular gate and stile, in the hedgerows on the left, which you need to climb and follow the path downfield towards hedgerows of hawthorn, alder and larch. A plank bridge and a lift-plank stile then take you across the pleasant stream, from which your path strikes upslope, towards the stile in the field corner near the private residence. Climb this stile, cross the private road and go over the stile opposite. Make your way along the path, crossing the crop or arable field. You are likely to see meadow pipits, skylark, linnets and pied wagtails. In the April-May breeding season you'll see cock pheasants drawing attention to themselves by crowing and wing-flapping.

Ahead is the boundary wall of Calke Park. When you reach the wall you will see the corner stile then, in the wall to the right, a handgate. Go through this, turn left along the path between the wall to your left and the deer enclosure fence to your right. Bracken and foxgloves clothe the pathside in summer and you may glimpse a spotted flycatcher or two. Calke has grazed herds of red and fallow deer for many years. The records for 1892 show it to have been grossly overstocked, the three hundred and twenty seven acres then being grazed by four hundred fallow deer and thirty red.

The sweeps of parkland which you see when you are travelling the formal lime tree avenue to Calke Abbey suggest that the deer could not have had a better setting. The weights given for both red and fallow were a good average yet, so far as a grazing programme was concerned, there was less than one acre of ground for each deer. Some artificial and winter feeding programme was operational, hence the existence of the deer barn. Nevertheless, in my opinion, fifty of each deer would have been adequate, and still as pleasing to the eye.

In the Abbey, deer heads are on display with plaques beneath indicating from which outlying wood the animal was shot. This is a sure indication that some of the red deer leaped that comparatively low wall to your left and existed for a time on the farmlands. It is not surprising, because to keep this deer species enclosed the fence or wall would need to be 6½-7 feet high.

Turn right, with the path and the deer enclosure still on your right. Follow the path downhill and round the corner to where the enclosure pool joins the outlying arm of Staunton Harold Reservoir. Notice the weir and the sweep of willows here. In all probability, there will be a heron on the fringes of the enclosure pool. Climb the stiles and follow the path, with the arm of water to your left. Pairs of great crested grebe, golden-eye, goosander and red-backed merganser can be identified through binoculars and 'scopes' in the autumn and winter.

Eventually the path swings away from the water's edge and bears uphill to the car park and viewpoint. You need now to be on the right, and facing oncoming traffic. That familiar car park foraging bird, the chaffinch, should be around in good numbers, and over the wall to your right are the slopes of Calke's deer and sheep paddocks. You will soon reach the vehicle entrance to Calke Abbey.

Here you can turn and divert to **Walk Three** or continue to Staunton Harold Hall, in which case you need still to be facing oncoming traffic. Beyond Calke's vehicle entrance notice the individual cottage styles and beware the occasional Jack Russell terrier. At the T-junction you need to turn left with care, then cross to the right so that you are again facing oncoming traffic. The imposing farmhouse on the corner was built in 1880. Notice the half-timbered front. Perhaps a previous house or coach-

Calke Abbey surrounded by lakes and parkland

ing inn was once established here. In March and April the ancient craft of hedge-layering takes place along this roadside. If I'm not mistaken, the ornamental tree by the silver birches and hawthorns on the left is a blue atlas cedar.

The road takes you over the reservoir and backwater to the car park, from where you will find a yellow signposted path leading up the banks and steps and through the hawthorns and brambles of Spring Wood. This is a permissive path.

Gradually the picturesque folds of land open up as you make your way onto the ridge via the stile and then turn right alongside a field with the boundary wall of Staunton Harold Hall on your right. Eventually, a railed gap in this wall will give you a view of the splendid lake which, in midsummer, nurtures some quite extensive water-lily beds. You will also see the hall and the oak avenue. From this point continue along the path to the stile gap in the corner wall. A left and right turn need to be made here, then you soon pass the monumental ruins of a once quite splendid oak, such as can be seen at Calke. This wooded tract is a good place to see woodpeckers, nuthatch and treecreepers. The yellow marker guides you down steps and over the field banks with the ornate entrance of Staunton Harold Hall now coming into view.

As you approach the road entrance, watch out for the traffic but also take in the green contours of undulating parkland. If you are pressed for time and do not intend to explore the grounds of this interesting country seat, go through the main gates between the two lakes, then bear left slightly to cross the lawns of the hall. Where the building ends, another right turn will take you to the Georgian courtyards which also house the Ferrers Centre. Continue by the courtyards then turn on a few pages to begin **Walk Three** which takes you back through Calke and onto the Staunton Harold Reservoir route.

For those intending to stay, read on...

Brief exploration of Staunton Harold Hall

The two animals rearing against the sky and positioned either side of the gate pillars are a four-antlered stag and a talbot. Originally these overlooked the formal garden entrance. The lake to your left is known as Church Pool and is leased by the Ryder Cheshire Foundation to the

Swadlincote Anglers Association. The fine sweep of water to your right is called the Serpentine and the near lawn bank only invites public scrutiny, for this privately-owned water holds the interests of another local angling syndicate.

If you turn your back temporarily on the hall and church, the parkland slopes on the opposite side of the water will catch your eye. The scattered and singular oaks suggest that this area was part of the original deerpark. What happened to the early deer herd seems to have remained unrecorded but in 1891 or 1892 one hundred fallow and ten red deer were re-introduced to Staunton Harold, probably having been acquired from the nearby estates of Calke or Castle Donington, and herded along the ridge and valley tracks by the deerkeepers of each estate. After the severe winter of 1935, however, the Staunton Harold deer records show 'nil' stock. So, in all probability, the deer may have escaped over or through the enclosure fences when the snowdrifts provided easy access. One local resident has informed me that a well-used tract of deerpark is now beneath the depths of Staunton Harold Reservoir.

The church was built in 1653, during Cromwell's Commonwealth. The plaque above the door mentions the church's founder, Sir Robert Shirley, but before his name, listed historically, is that of Harold the Saxon who is believed to have been the estate's first owner. He lost it to Henry de Ferraris; a recipient chosen by William the Conqueror. Eventually, the name changed, probably during Queen Anne's reign, to Earl Ferrers.

In 1423, however, the Shirleys acquired the estate through marriage and Sir Robert Shirley was titled a baron, with the signature of Charles II distinguishing the appropriate scroll. The church, with the original box pews, fine panelling and painted ceiling is worth a visit. There is also a chancel screen made from wrought-iron, various hangings, cushions and the Shirley family monuments.

Staunton Harold Hall includes structures designed for the two previous houses which stood on the site. The style of the present house is Palladian. How the building reverted from a family home, won the interest of Group Captain Leonard Cheshire and became the Sue Ryder Palliative Care Home is described on information plaques and leaflets.

If you make your way from the church towards that narrow belt of woodland, notice on the lawn corner to the right the stone marking the resting place of *'Bogey, her Ladyship's black pug, died 1902 aged 12'.* Maybe other Victorian or Edwardian pets are buried close by.

Paths through the woodland belt known as The Wilderness eventually turn alongside the reeded end of Church Pool. Here a stand of bamboo suggests that a duck decoy was once established. Today, there is a chance of seeing reed bunting, reed warbler and kingfisher. After connecting the banks of the two lakes, turn towards the hall and the Sue Ryder car park, to the Georgian courtyards and stable block where the duck decoymen would have conferred with woodsmen, deerkeepers and estate workers in rooms used today by the craftsfolk of the Ferrers Centre.

For twenty five years or so, craftspeople have been displaying and selling their wares in the previously derelict buildings which were restored with that purpose in mind. The coffee is very good here too. Gardening enthusiasts will delight in the walled gardens, privately-owned and recorded as being one of the earliest garden centres to become established. It is sought out by enthusiasts, amateurs and experts alike, travelling from the suburbs of the surrounding cities.

An eye catching arrangement of trees: Staunton Harold

Walk Three:

Duration: Approx 1/2-3/4 hour before reaching Calke

The Route

Begin from this stable block and the periphery road leading to Heath End. It is fairly direct but if you are uncertain, enquire at the centre.

On the road you will pass Hunt House and the aptly named Park View. Go through the white gate with the wall to your right, and limes and oaks flanking the roadside. Study the view over to your left. Trees — in this case mostly oaks — were planted to serve as field and enclosure boundary markers. After the gate and cattle grid, you can continue down the wide grass verge and follow the signposts marked Calke or embark on this next interesting diversion.

When the hedge to your right ends, turn right and walk over the undulating grassland, still with the hedge on your right. Notice the wooded tract of oak, lime and larch over to your left. At the stile is a yellow waymarker. The path is well-defined and takes you by stands of ash, rowan and self-regenerated sycamore. The usual umbellifers and ground ivy fringe the route and a few mature beech come into sight.

At the next fence, turn right. There is a wooded valley on your left. The path takes you upslope and down, following the fence and hedge line. Silver birch fringe the reedy pool to your left, and ahead notice how well-planned and renovated the path has become. If you are a photographer, consider the stand of Scots pine on the field skyline to your right. Although the path dips, there are still viewpoints of the pool and silver birch valley to your left.

Continue and climb the path steps, and enjoy the sequestered Laundry Pool opening up on your left. The site was quarried by the Earls Ferrers, lime having been the prime extraction. The Severn Trent interpretive notice mentions eleven more lime kilns, and some of the expected species to be seen about this next woodland tract known as the Dimminsdale Nature Reserve. Not surprisingly, the kingfisher can occasionally be seen darting across the surface of these pools.

After you have become accustomed to the boarded walks taking you over the ditches, you will meet with the main road ahead — the road already walked. My advice here is to cross with care, face oncoming traffic and walk back to the Calke T-junction, where you need to turn right carefully and cross when you reach the vehicle exit to Calke Abbey. Re-enter Calke, walk again facing oncoming traffic and with Home Farm on your right. Sheep and ponies graze the paddocks here, and there are usually geese and ducks on the pond. On my first walk here I was surprised to see a pond-bound mute swan displaying and posturing to one of the domestic geese! Once you are through the handgate and over the cattle grid, St. Giles church dominates. Inside is a splendid monument to Sir John Harpur and his wife.

Over to your left, stand the ruins of the deer barn which, as you can see, was built to last. Such buildings was used for the storage of foodstuffs such as hay, mangolds and swedes on which deer are usually fed during the winter. They also facilitated culling. The old Victorian or Edwardian deerkeeper would position himself here with a shotgun and cull the selected deer while they were feeding.

Calke Abbey — its orangery, and outbuildings now serving as toilet blocks, restaurant and interpretive centre — can hardly be missed to your right. It is worth pausing in your walk for a look round here, if only to become aware of the commendable restoration programme which National Trust employees and volunteers have undertaken in recent years.

To continue your walk, you need to have your back to the abbey and to cross the car park, with the deerpark slopes and a Dutch-type barn to your right. In the last car park, swing left towards the low post-and-rail fence, go through the handgate at the wall boundary corner, then follow the fence down towards the chain of lakes. Swing left with the path for a few yards, then go down the steps with the water on your left. Look for the herons preening on the tree branches. A few feral mallard, coot, moorhen and a pair of little grebe may be seen. Both oaks and waterside alders are noticeable here, and a few old, deeply-rooted beech. The chain of ponds are known as Betty's Pond (near the entrance drive), Thatch House Pond and Nene Pond (which we are walking alongside). In the deer paddock are the China House and Little Dog Kennel Ponds.

Waterlilies provide an interesting surface carpet in summer. On some country estates, in Victorian and Edwardian times, waterlilies were harvested and wax-coated so that they could be used to decorate coffins.

The fence on your right is the deer paddock boundary. To your left is a strangely-shaped beech. Where the path turns, you will see the landrover

Hedge layering with blue atlas cedar and silver birches near Calke Abbey

track passing along the enclosure's edge. Both the red and fallow deer are freshly-introduced stock. The fallow vary in colour, being spotted or menil, brownish-grey, or 'common coloured' — white and black strains prevalent among them. Black fallow are thought to have been introduced to this country from Norway by the hunt-conscious King James I. The menil may well have been introduced by the Romans. They certainly do without water for a considerable time compared to the red and sika deer, so it may be that the fallow evolved in the Asiatic countries but have adapted well over here.

Over to the left, the slopes are clothed with bracken, and in summer, with foxgloves. One Christmas holiday morning of freezing fog and white encasing hoar-frost, friends and I flushed a dog-fox from his lie up here, and on returning two days later we gained a close up of two goldcrests intently scouring the tree bark for torpid insect life.

Upon the path beside the boundary wall you need to make a decision, for you are close to the handgate and the fieldpaths along which you need to retrace your steps to the Staunton Harold car park and the end of the walk. You can make your way back from here but for a future exploration of the parkland, turn left and go down the bracken slopes and between the oaks if you intend to leave by the Ticknall entrance. Notice the old stag-headed oaks, small tracts of which still connect South Derbyshire to the Needwood Forest country; small tracts which suggest that the Great Derbyshire Forest once extended for many more miles than we often realise.

Many of Calke's trees are individual in shape and character — sweet chestnuts with twisted trunks, some really old specimens of beech, lime, ash, larch, cedar and various pines — all of which have led to this wooded parkland area being designated a Site of Special Scientific Interest.

The National Trust wardens also encourage visitors to call in at the lambing marquee.

Brief History of the Sheep Flocks

From the National Trust warden accompanying those of us who attended a New Year guided walk led by former MP for South Derbyshire, Edwina Currie, I took notes outlining the history of the Calke Abbey sheep breeds.

The sheep breed which has been connected to Calke since 1720 is the Portland. These sheep are believed to have been first recorded as living a feral existence around Portland Bill in Dorset. They are said to have swum ashore when a Spanish galleon struck a rock outcrop a short distance away. Whether this is legend or fact, no-one knows. If the original Portlands were from the galleon, they would have been transported as food cargo. On hearing of the breed, a member of the Harpur family arranged for a small flock to be transported to Calke. They arrived in 1720 and by 1886, over four hundred Portlands were grazing the extensive parklands.

When Sir John died, he decreed that Portlands should always be kept at Calke but, by 1956, only thirty remained. Since 1991 the flock has been built up to include one hundred breeding ewes and the entire flock are purebred.

Calke's commercial sheep flock currently consists of three hundred and fifty breeding mule ewes and nine or ten Suffolk rams, the descendants of a flock founded twenty to twenty-five years ago.

Calke Abbey

Recommended reading: The National Trust — *Calke Abbey, Derbyshire: A Hidden House Revealed* by Howard Colvin.

General information:
Calke Park is open throughout the year and, as previously stated, there is a charge for vehicles, although National Trust members are allowed free access.

House, Gardens and Church:
Open from Saturday to Wednesday from April to October.

Shop and Restaurant:
The same days as the house but from 11.00am–5.00pm.
Christmas Shop and Restaurant open at weekends from November to mid-December from noon–4.00pm.

Why not call at Swarkestone Bridge...

Swarkestone is best known for its bridge, extending for three-quarters of a mile across the Trent floodplain. Built in the thirteenth century, with a chapel incorporated in the main structure, the bridge connected Swarkestone with Stanton by Bridge.

Restored in the early part of the nineteenth century, the bridge we see today has seventeen arches, four main ones spanning the uncertain currents of the Trent.

In 1643 Sir John Pell won a skirmish with a Cavalier troop at Swarkestone, and in 1745 the vanguard of Prince Charles Edward Stuart's army came here but decided that the planned march on London could not go ahead.

What to do at Swarkestone? There is a popular hostelry here and, on the Weston and Aston side of the Trent, an interesting walk from Swarkestone back along the towpath of the Trent and Mersey Canal. The fields around the bridge, which were once part of the floodplain, have been reclaimed and are now used for arable farming. Local flooding problems have also been eased by gravel extraction contractors. A yachting club is very prominent and a kayak club meets by the bridge buttress rapids on most Sunday mornings.

From a double-decker bus you can see the small reedy pools circling the bridge buttresses. Such pools attract the snipe, reed bunting and coot pairs which breed there. The occasional pair of mute swans lead their cygnets from pool to pool so that they can feed on the surface weed for several months before the adults escort them to the river.

Hard weather brings in the pochard, tufted duck and wigeon which graze the field in good numbers.

Exploring the Erewash and Nottingham Canals

M1 Junction: 26 for the A610

Start: The Great Northern Basin,
Derby Road, Langley Mill, Derbys

Car Parking: Cossall — Lay-by beside canal
Langley Mill — the hardstanding on the opposite side of the road

Buses: From Victoria Centre Nottingham — Trent
R1 Langley Mill (Great Northern)
From Derby — 120 and 125

Refreshments: The Great Northern, Langley Mill
The Bridge Inn, Cotmanhay

Distance: 4½ miles

Duration: 3-3½ hours steady walking

About the walk:
The theme of this exploration is 'contrasts'. Beginning at the termination point of both the Erewash and Nottingham canals, one can see how a bygone industrial age still clings to the bridges, locks and waterside buildings of the Erewash Canal. Then, by changing to the ridgetop course of the Nottingham Canal at Cossall, it becomes apparent how a disused waterway can serve as a natural reserve for many interesting varieties of plant, amphibian, bird and small mammal life. If you choose to follow the

towpaths at the weekend you will find yourself sharing them with cyclists, particularly by the Erewash Canal, and occasional horse riders along the Nottingham Canal towpath.

The best way of exploring this interesting route is to form a group for whom two or more cars can provide a shuttle service, with one or more vehicles parked in the lay-by at Cossall and the others being driven the six miles or so through Cossall village and on to the A610 Kimberley/ Eastwood bypass, continuing to Langley Mill as the signs indicate. Keep the scrubland and industrial sites on your left more or less all the way and ignore the signs to Eastwood, while following those clearly marked 'Langley Mill'.

Once you have turned left at the last island, on to Derby Road, the Great Northern Basin and white-fronted pub of the same name are soon to be seen on your right.

The Great Northern Basin

Begin at the Great Northern Basin, built by William Jessop in 1796. By the lockgate and towpath, note that this wharf and interchanging point was intentionally channelled so that the Nottingham and Cromford canals were linked with the Erewash, and the transportation of northern coal was made as smooth an operation as possible at the time. When the canal closed, the basin filled gradually with coal slurry washed in from Moorgreen Reservoir. A group of canal and boating enthusiasts founded what has since become the Erewash Canal Preservation and Development Association. The basin was finally re-opened in 1973. Unfortunately, the Cromford and Nottingham canals termination points had to be closed due to mining subsidence but a friendly member of the Association told me that the Cromford connection may be re-opened within the next four years.

Today, the basin provides both long-term and overnight moorings, winter storage facilities, a boat repair and engine sales business, slipway, dry dock, crane and boat-building wharf. If you attend a rally here you will find yourself in genial company and, no doubt, meet watercolour artists displaying their work alongside such craftspeople as potters, woodturners and picture framing experts. We have the hard-working members of the Association to thank for making our exploration possible by having restored the basin, its lock gates and towpath.

The lockgates nearest to the road bridge were removed from the Wollaton section of the Nottingham Canal when the colliery stretch was closed in the late 1960s. As a boy I spent many summer evenings beside these structures, without realising that I would meet with the same set of lock gates on my exploration of the Langley Mill Basin some thirty years later. A brief history of the Erewash Canal can be found on page 56.

The Route

From the basin, pass carefully beneath the road bridge and continue down the towpath. There are usually a few anglers within sight of the bridge. Notice the arrowhead waterplants bedded here and also the width of the canal — much wider than the Cromford and sections of Nottingham Canal. Either side are allotments and filterbeds. You are never entirely free of an industrialised landscape. But keep walking! The alders and willows on the first bends look splendid in mid-October, as do the oaks rising from the hedgerows.

Here, in autumn, I have seen a swan pair flying towards the Derbyshire/Leicestershire border, and a splendid and colourful file of narrowboats from Stoke on Trent, Gainsborough and Barton-under-Needwood, cleaving the water as they were steered towards a rally at the basin. Just as Eastwood Lock comes into sight, so too do the fields to the right. Here the sunlight enhances the masses of buttercups and celandines. Cowslips were probably abundant in D.H. Lawrence's time. His early novels evolved from such meadowscapes, although the first chapters of *Sons and Lovers* were set in the streets and houses of the hilly mining town of Eastwood, where Lawrence was born at 8a Victoria Street.

At Eastwood Lock you need to cross the lock, to the opposite towpath. There are many small mammals such as voles and mice on the broken-up field tracts out to the left, and the occasional weasel or family of weasels can be seen hunting here. One evening six of these little russet predators passed within inches of my walking boots.

You are also likely to see linnets, goldfinches, greenfinches, long-tailed tits, starlings, pied wagtails and meadow-pipits. Moorhens ferry along and around the reed fringes.

Shipley Lock and Bridge are ahead. Notice too the different buildings rising beyond the trees — farmhouses and yards mostly and the traditional mill-house with its adjacent storage sheds.

A few yards on you will reach an aqueduct, with the lively flow of the River Erewash glittering and shimmering below. Look for a kingfisher because the water is relatively shallow and the alder, ash and willow branches provide perches. You may also see pied and grey wagtails and siskin feeding here, usually in the autumn and winter.

Close to the canal is the old slaughterhouse where injured pit ponies and work-jaded narrowboat horses were put down. It is now a homestead.

A pen once collided with an overhead cable near here, then settled with her mate on the canal. By feeding grain to the swans, a friend of mine was able to lift the startled and hissing pen from the water. She had one or two displaced flight feathers, so he decided to keep her in a hay-filled stable overnight, then called in someone from the RSPCA the following morning.

The word 'mute' is a misnomer as far as this swan species is concerned, as my friend discovered when darkness fell. The pen called consistently to her mate throughout the night and he answered her every intonation. My friend got very little sleep! When the swan's wing was examined the next morning it was found to be intact. There was no injury to the joint, so the pen was returned to the canal and her waiting mate.

The next canal stretch is justifiably feted by anglers. Note the shape of the reedbed by the opposite bank. This was undoubtedly a wharf, perhaps where agricultural produce was occasionally handled. Again, the willows and alders could produce a kingfisher. I have glimpsed one here. It is just a question of being around at the right time.

Pass beneath the railway bridge. Opening up on your left is a nature reserve, created by digging out spoil to maintain satisfactory anchorage for the railway embankment. As usual, water has found its level here and waterplant spores were probably brought in on the paddles of visiting swans and mallard. Coot pairs will be nesting in March and April and you will recognise reed buntings, particularly in the winter when you may also see and hear a water rail.

The high screen of stalks is made up of phragmites, which attract not only kingfishers but the reed-warbler pairs which nest here, despite the presence of anglers. In the late summer, swallows, house martins, wagtails and starlings roost and, as you would expect, the territorial mute swan pair have hatched cygnets. One retired Cotmanhay miner told me how he cycled daily for twenty-nine years along this stretch of towpath and never an April went by without him having seen a swan incubating on a high-piled nest. Possibly two or three swan pairs spanned that length of time but the recent breeding pair are closer to the Bridge Inn and round the wide bend.

October Sunday morning at Eastwood Lock

(T. Stevenson Collection)

One relatively young pair broke habitat tradition by overlooking the phragmites water and nesting on the opposite side of the canal which is, in fact, an island, there being a long reeded channel of water behind it. When their cygnets need to feed on surface weed, the cob and pen take them on to this channel and people often pass by without realising there are swans in the vicinity. Moorhens are here, naturally, but the vegetation between the houses and the canal attracts an interesting summer migrant, heard more often than seen. This is the grasshopper-warbler which can be heard reeling deep into the dusk in May and June.

Over to your left you will eventually see a rough path crossing the field and making towards the railway tunnel, beyond which the River Erewash winds through the fields. If you are a bird-watcher it is sometimes worth leaving the towpath for a few minutes, because on the canal side of the railway embankment another narrow tract of water is screened by haw, alder and willow thicket. As well as the titmice species you may glimpse, in winter, siskin seeking the alder cones, while the summer yield usually consists of redpoll, whinchat and spotted flycatcher. A sparrowhawk may be seen, while beyond the railway bridge a kestrel pair patrol over the fields.

The Bridge Inn at Cotmanhay is worth a visit. Its regulars are friendly and its bar surroundings hung with replica pistols or inlaid with interesting aquariums. Often there is a narrowboat moored nearby. The nearby sign informs you of the distance you have covered — as yet, only two and a quarter miles. Over to your left is a trace of scrubland inlaid with paths and sometimes a long-tethered pony or two grazing. Beyond it is a coal washing plant. Follow the low hedgerow to where a shale path cuts off to the left.

Leave the canal towpath and follow this path to the wooden steps of the railway bridge, which you need to cross, noticing the River Erewash down on the left. The path continues inside a fenced area and passes beneath the Bennerley Viaduct. Over on the left, the River Erewash continues to wind low between fields sloping down from the ridge, along which runs the Nottingham Canal.

Continue along this path with the railway to your right. Eventually the path and fence meet with the lane. This is as good a place as any to pause and take stock of your present surroundings. These fields, for instance, are feeding grounds for flocks of lapwing and golden plover. Redshank,

Notice for narrowboatmen at Langley Mill Basin signed by "Donk"
(T. Stevenson Collection)

snipe, whimbrel and woodcock are also recorded here. Wild mallard, teal and tufted duck stop by, as well as summer migrants like the wheatear. In winter there are flocks of fieldfare and redwing.

Railwaymen working on the track at night have heard wigeon, that far-travelling duck from the north, whistling constantly as they feed across the soaking grasses. Today you may only see a sizeable flock of farm ducks and the geese trooping to or from the farm on the lane side corner. But be assured, this is indeed a wealthy wildlife habitat.

Do not disregard the Bennerley Viaduct. This was completed in 1877, stability being the most important consideration throughout its planning and design. A structure was needed that would serve in crossing five hundred yards of precarious ground caverned beneath the surface with both ironstone tunnellings and coal extract workings. Water meadows, the Erewash river and canal, the Midland Railway, and the nearby Nottingham Canal posed a further threat, wrought iron was decided upon for the viaduct, and a 'warren' style of design which featured lattice. This design had been patented in 1848.

No further serious problems relating to the ground conditions existed for the shareholders and passengers of the Great Northern Railway. The line was finally closed in 1968. Fortunately, though, this splendid structure is now Grade Two listed, which is reason enough for us to view it today.

Leaving the viaduct, continue along the little fenced path, taking you safely off the busy road connecting the bypass to Cotmanhay and Ilkeston. The River Erewash passes beneath the road. Notice the 'mermaid hair' trails of green weed here and, in the late dusk, settle with binoculars to watch the birds feeding on the fields.

One raw June evening, I watched a dog-fox systematically quartering sections of the field as he hunted for newly-hatched lapwing chicks. Grown lapwings repeatedly mobbed him but he appeared oblivious to their presence as he trotted swiftly, muzzle to the ground and russet coat blazing against the grass.

The fenced path takes us gently alongside the poultry-foraged field. My last count of the farmyard ducks grazing here came to thirty-seven. Where the path ends, cross the road and go through the handgate, alongside which the marker *Nottingham Canal Trail* is positioned. Now you are walking beside the waterway once known to bygone lengthmen as 'top cut', whereas the Erewash Canal back there was "t'bottom cut". Between March and May you will probably pass a pair of old mute swans nesting on the bank just below the towpath level. Why they choose to nest here when, on the opposite side, there are reed clumps and overgrown banks with orchard gardens, is anyone's guess.

When the cygnets hatch, this pair spend only a few days with them on the canal before leading the brood in file down the field to the River Erewash, which they use as a feeding ground until the cygnets are fledged in the autumn. The cob carries a dark blue leg-ring which shows he was hatched in Cheshire. I have noted these colour rings fitted to the legs of most swans foraging along the Dee at Chester. Swans ringed in Nottinghamshire now carry the yellow-banded 'Darvic' ring. The pen, however, is probably a locally-hatched bird for quite a number of female cygnets return to breed on or close to their place of birth. She has probably not flown further than the Attenborough Gravels reserve which is where many young pre-breeding swans meet and begin pairing. Within days of the adults having escorted the 1997 brood down to the Erewash, they vanished, and I suspect the dog-fox may have been responsible for their disappearance.

When you have crossed the by-pass (now furnished with pedestrian, equestrian and toad-crossing signs), you just need to continue along the towpath. However, diverting briefly at the piped aqueduct, and another mile or so will take you back to the Cossall lay-by where you will cross the footbridge to find your car waiting.

For this stretch of the canal walk a seasonal guide follows.

The Spring Walk

Moorhen and coot pairs will be nesting and rearing broods. Little grebe may visit but often the footpath on both sides is a disturbance factor and they seldom breed except at Cossall Forks. Swallows and house martins hawk for flies. All the usual small woodland and hedgerow birds may be seen and heard, especially whitethroat, lesser whitethroat and yellowhammer. By late April and into May, butterflies seen include the common blue, meadow brown, small skipper, red admiral, peacock and small tortoiseshell.

The net-dippers I have spoken with assure me that pond skaters, water boatmen and the great diving beetle abound here. Frog- and toad-spawn and tadpoles usually proliferate and the mute swans and mallard seek the spawn, which they relish.

The Summer Walk

Conservationists enthuse about the diversity of water plants such as the yellow iris, water-plantain, branched bur-reed and reed-mace, while admitting that the Japanese knotweed, if left unchecked, could become a problem. In late summer, look for the dragonflies and damsel flies.

The Autumn Walk

In the early autumn, whinchat and redstart may be glimpsed as they embark upon their migration flights. Small groups of goldfinch and greenfinch seek the seedheads. Two or three herons fish here and stretch or preen in the fields on the opposite side. When the hips and haws are burnished and clustered along the hedgerows, fieldfares and redwings will gather to feed.

The Winter Walk

Pairs or small groups of tufted duck fly in to feed at first light. Pied and grey wagtails are likely to be seen. Snipe, grey plover and lapwings will be feeding or wheeling over the field. The mute swan cygnets will be indulging in their circular flights. The adult swans may eventually leave with them and fly to the flocking area on Attenborough Gravels or elsewhere in the Trent Valley. Other swans may fly in to feed or indulge in pairing behaviour patters, but these will be driven off when the breeding residents return.

The banks of freezing fog and the swans create an ethereal effect, which I first experienced when I bypassed a pair drifting on the canal surface. Such an effect is always worth photographing.

The Great Northern Pub

If you intend returning to Langley Mill, do explore the waterway cottage area at the rear of the Great Northern pub, then call in and sample the beer, food and the cosiness of the windowside alcoves. A few framed canal scenes are usually on display and the atmosphere is very enjoyable.

The Erewash Canal — a brief history

John Varley is the engineer who constructed the Erewash Canal, which was completed in 1779. It is a waterway containing fifteen locks and extending for 11¾ miles. It was linked closely with the Derby, Nutbrook, Cromford and Nottingham canals and, from the shareholders' viewpoint, was a successful proposition. There was no need to build an intensive flight of locks and trade, whether it be coal, quarried stone or night-soil, was brisk until the formation of the railway system. By 1932, this waterway had become part of the Grand Union Canal system.

Fortunately, the continuing interest in pleasure boating ensured that the waterway remained navigable despite the closure, in 1962, of the stretch from Gallows Inn, Ilkeston to Langley Mill, allegedly by the administrators of the British Transport Commission, to be succeeded by the British Waterways Board. By 1968 a public meeting was held in protest at this canal being regarded as 'a remainder waterway'. As a result of the concern shared amongst all the participants of that meeting, the Erewash Canal Preservation and Development Association was gradually, but enthusiastically, formed and its members were successful in persuading the Nottinghamshire and Derbyshire County Councils to share the costs of maintaining the waterway with the British Waterways Board. This agreement was reached by 1972 and, as a cruising, angling and towpath-walking amenity, the canal is now a unique asset to the social and cultural scene.

The Nottingham Canal — a brief history

The estimated cost of this waterway had been in the region of fifty thousand pounds. By the time of its completion, another thirty thousand had been added to the bill.

William Jessop, its famed engineer, had designed the all-important Wollaton stretch to begin at a cutting-in along the Beeston section and progress through what is now the Lenton Abbey estate, then on up to Wollaton. However, one of the most important shareholders, Lord Middleton, disapproved of this idea. His proposed and accepted route entailed building fifteen extra lock gates which became known as 'The Wollaton Flight' and it was the installation of these that created the extra costs. Opened in 1796, the canal length was $14\frac{3}{4}$ miles with coal being the usual cargo, although agricultural produce, quarried stone and, in later years, crated consignments of tinned food were transported along this waterway.

By 1928, due to the success of the railways, canal transport was no longer considered a viable proposition. The canal was closed and, in 1937, finally abandoned. Forty years later it became council property and is a nature reserve.

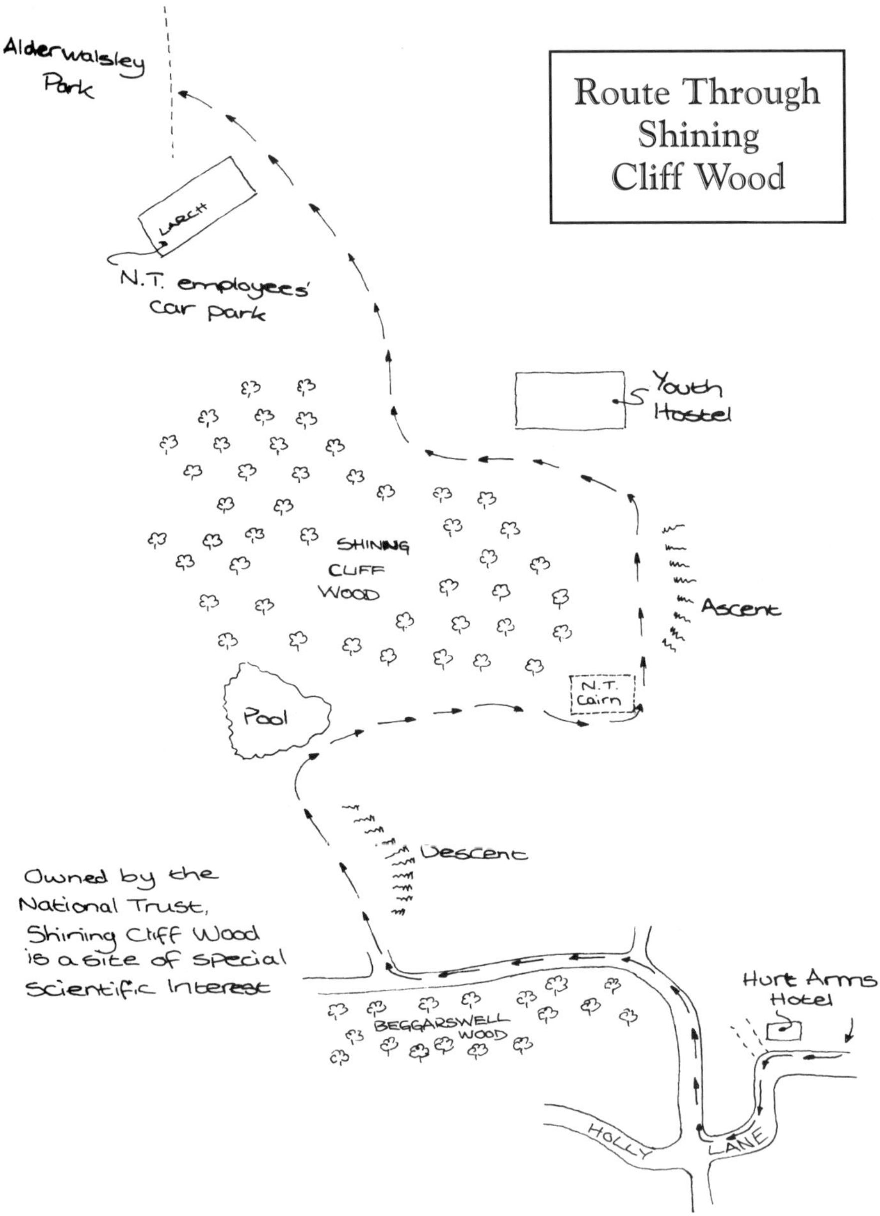
Route Through Shining Cliff Wood
Alderwalsley Park
LARCH
N.T. employees' car park
Youth Hostel
SHINING CLIFF WOOD
Ascent
N.T. Cairn
Pool
Descent
Owned by the National Trust, Shining Cliff Wood is a site of special Scientific Interest
BEGGARSWELL WOOD
Hurt Arms Hotel
HOLLY LANE

Cromford Canal and Shining Cliff Wood

M1 Junction:	28 for Alfreton & Matlock A38
Start:	Cromford Canal Wharf Car Park Old Wharf, Mill Lane, Cromford
Car Parking:	Turn right off the A6 into Mill Road. It may be signposted as the 'Arkwright Mill Car Park' and is situated on the right.
Buses:	Transpeak from Nottingham and Derby. Alight at Cromford, cross the road to Mill Lane.
Refreshments:	The Derwent Arms, Whatstandwell
Distance:	First section: 2¾ miles; Second walk: 7.1 miles
Duration:	First section: 1½ hours; Second walk: 3¾ hours

About the walk

Like other walks in this book, this exploration can be regarded as three separate walks or one long walk covering about 9½ miles which, with a refreshment stop and a look round all points of interest, will take the best part of a day.

The route is interesting and worth photographing at all times of the year, but May and June are the months for seeing and enjoying the splendour of the limestone flowers. You may well encounter mud after rain, especially in Shining Cliff Wood so adequate footwear needs to be worn. It is not a difficult track by any stretch of the imagination, but the wood contours keep you in trim and contrast pleasantly with the flat walking experienced while exploring the canal towpath.

I have not provided a map for the canal trail but I have attempted to guide you through Shining Cliff Wood as comfortably as possible.

References to Cromford, High Peak Railway, Willersley Castle and Lea Hurst will be found at the end of this section.

The Route

Cromford Wharf's grassy areas attract the feral mallard, chaffinch and pied wagtail in to feed. Hawfinches can be seen foraging here in late autumn and early winter. In May and June, on a sunlit morning, blackbirds flute, moorhens and mallard ferry across the canal surface with their broods. Jackdaws converse in the pines, beeches and silver birches. Forget-me-nots enhance the towpath trail.

Leave the car park and walk with the canal on your right. You will not go far before glimpsing a water vole foraging along the opposite bank, or swimming to its burrow beneath this nearside bank. You can occasionally follow one for quite a few yards beneath the tussocky edges of the waterway where the entrances to its several underwater burrows are situated. In many parts of Britain water voles are on the decline but fortunately not here on the Cromford Canal. Mink, the wanton killers of all small mammals and birds, are thought to be responsible for the voles' depletion.

Notice the pleasant water meadows down on the left, a good place to see snipe and redshank. Beyond the accommodation bridge, oaks, willows, haw and blackthorn can be seen. Scan the relatively clear canal bed for small pike and, in May, look out for orange-tip butterflies. You will see water being piped into the canal as it teems down from the hills, seeking its own level.

In the autumn and winter glass the stands of alder for the siskin flocks exploring the cones. Brambling are not unknown here and you may glimpse a grey wagtail or two. As you close in on the High Peak Junction Museum, look at the surfaces of the partly submerged stones close to the water's edge and you will see the droppings of water voles on some, and the scatterings of food remains on others. In April and May you may even glimpse a mallard egg deposited or 'cached' among the aquatic weed by voles or brown rats.

There are stone-built filter beds over to the left and you can cross the canal to learn about the High Peak Junction at the museum. There is also a well-stocked gift shop. Notice the tall chimney confirming the whereabouts of the Leawood and Middleton pumping station. There is a moss-sided horse trough close to the wall a few yards on, with the tether rope still attached. On the opposite side of the canal, Lea Hurst can be seen — the home of Florence Nightingale.

When you reach the aqueduct taking the canal over the fast-flowing River Derwent, notice how the waterway has narrowed. Designed by William Jessop, this is known as a 'single span' aqueduct. In the wooded valley below I saw nine splendid trout caught by mayfly bait and a mallard leaving her beautiful down-filled nest in the crock of a willow. Inside the nest were fourteen eggs, one of which was chipping.

Notice the size and age difference of the alder and ash trees fringing the Derwent. The two derelict cottages were probably home to the canal lengthmen and their families, and it is worth pausing here to reflect on their lives.

Continue along the towing path; high, steep, contour woodland over on the left and a valley of damp rambling woodland to your right. A notice here informs you that this is a Derbyshire Wildlife Trust Reserve. In late April and early May, the blackcap and woodwarbler cocks will be singing. You may hear pheasant and, at dusk, the woodcock males begin their crepuscular flights of 'roding' or marking out their territorial boundaries.

At the next aqueduct, notice how the aquatic weed has so successfully colonised the shallows. The canal here passes over the railway. In late April and May, bluebells and pink and white campion cover the banks and wooded slopes and, over on the left, oak and silver birch merge with the alders and willows. In May, inhale the scent of the ramsons or wild garlic, with its masses of white-flowered heads. Usually, a pair of little grebe, or dabchick, will be preening or foraging through the surface weed as you near the long tunnel. Continue along this and notice Crich Tower on the skyline ahead.

When you have negotiated the Gregory Tunnel, pause to look at the reed bed, known as Gregory Dam. The heads of the mallard drakes are distinct from the greens of the surrounding vegetation and here is another good place to have a binocular view of another pair of little grebe or dabchick. If you are fortunate enough to have bright sunlight, check the grebe's dark brown back, dark blue head top, red eye and deep chestnut cheeks, neck and crop — beautiful! Notice now the holly and poplars contrasting with the oaks and silver birches. On the right we pass Lea Shaw Farm with its accommodation bridge. At path-level, the green-mossed stones and boulders screened by campion and nettles indicate how the foundation structures of the house and outbuildings have been built up from the towpath level.

Carry on for another quarter-of-a-mile or so, bypassing the splendid green-lawned residence on the opposite side. There are reeds, feral mallard with their broods and, as you near the Whatstandwell Bridge, you will hear the rooks clamouring from their nests before you see them. Now is as good a time and place as any to seek liquid refreshment so at the bridge, turn right and follow the pavement down to the Derwent Arms. It is a surprisingly spacious and very welcoming hostelry, with rams' horns and a yoke displayed along the rafters and interesting prints and paintings adorning the walls. There is also a small beer garden with an aviary containing budgerigars and parakeets.

When you return to the canal bridge, a choice of direction awaits you. You can either retrace your steps along the towpath to Cromford Wharf — or continue along the canal, often to the full-voiced crowing of a nearby cockerel. Sometimes there is a small gaggle of geese on this next canal stretch, which I find slightly less interesting than the one we have just walked, although in May the plant life compensates for this.

The far bank is again wooded, but on this towpath side, stands of meadowsweet may be seen, and on and around the walls, the pink flowers of the herb robert invite careful and gentle scrutiny. You will no doubt identify yellow archangel, one of the wildflower book labiates (hemp and dead nettles). The butterflies you are likely to encounter are common blue, orange-tip, small tortoiseshell and peacock. Look for siskin and brambling through the colder months and, when you are in the region of the small filter beds to the right, pick out from the meadowsweet occasional ramsons and white campion, the long-petalled flowers of the fieldmouse ear, which under favourable limestone conditions last from April to August.

Common vetch should also be flowering by April and May. Notice the bracken fronds thriving on the ivy-clad wall. The bugle with its hairy stem and powder-blue flowers also brightens the pathside from April to June. Tall branches sweep over the water here, particularly alder, sycamore and oak, and you may glimpse any of the three woodpecker species, nuthatch or treecreeper. Kingfishers use the low branches as prey-locating points, although I have not yet seen one of these splendid little birds along the Cromford Canal. Look out for one.

When the accommodation bridge comes into sight, you may see a water vole or two. Notice their trails through the reed stems. Fox scent is often strong along here and a vixen probably has a litter of cubs earthed somewhere along this railway bank. On the right beside the bridge, several grey stone cottages stand with front doors opening onto the towpath. Beneath the bridge the lawns of a fine private residence slope to the waters edge. There is another reed bed, or basin, and old wharf further along. On the right is a farm with parkland fields and woods over on the left as the next bridge comes into sight. This is where you leave the canal.

Turn right onto the road, walk down the lane and beneath the railway bridge. At the T-junction bear left and cross onto the right-hand pavement. Proceed to the next T-junction. The Little Chef should be to your left; the Hurt Arms Hotel on your right. Turn right onto Derby Road and, as the sign informs you, into the District of Amber Valley. After a recreation ground and what appears to be a chapel, turn right into Holly Lane. Face the oncoming traffic.

Cross the Derwent Bridge and the Derwent cut-off between the sycamores. Turn right and follow the wide direct track up by the private residences and on into Shining Cliff Wood. Begin to climb the winding uphill track, on either side of which are stands of sycamore, oak and the occasional holly. There are gardens surrounding the private residences. Foxes and tawny owls can be heard at night as well as rabbits and badgers. In May and June, freshly-foliaged silver birch, bracken fronds and masses of long-stemmed bluebells surround the green-mossed tree trunks. Gradually, a few pines come into view. White campion fringes the trackside and the strong scent of ramsons must drift beyond the doorsteps of those fortunate enough to be living close by.

The track surface appears to have been overlaid with limestone and granite chippings. Eventually, you will arrive at a right-hand fork which plunges steeply downhill. Descend this with care, especially after rain. It appears to be an old trackway, dipping and lifting. In the valley bottom is a sizeable pool. Turn right, with the water on your left.

A yard or two down, the watercourse invites the photographer to pause, particularly in May and early June. Here, the running water glistens as it washes over the stones. Green bracken fronds, bluebells and the stems of long grasses fringe the sides. Continue along the woodland path and, at the indicator cairn, turn left and proceed along the path towards the ridgetop. This is as good a place as any to see or hear one of the jays which breed in the wood.

The track continues up to the Youth Hostel nestled alongside a wall of rock. Notice the loose rocks close by. Keep the hostel on your right. Because of the ground flora and tree variations, this is a delightful ridge to explore, with different types and shapes of oaks, long grass and foxgloves. Eventually you will reach a small parking area used by the tree-felling and path-maintenance teams. Cross this, keeping the small plantations of larch to your left. Bear right here and continue to the wall corner. After passing through the farm gate proceed with the wall on your right. Notice the information sign indicating that you are now walking a section of the Midshires Way.

Ahead of you is a wide stand of tall silver birches and pines. Follow the track across the grass to the next tubular gate and the small walled wood on your left. Notice the lichens on top of the drystone wall. If you have a dog running ahead, call and secure it now because there are usually sheep grazing the fields ahead, through which you are permitted to pass. The track bypasses a larch stand, and on the right, the view of high-ridged woodland and lush parklands with the hamlet of Alderwasley nestling between will hold your gaze.

At the next tubular gate, a wooden pedestrian entrance has been erected alongside. There is a stock fence on your right. This is Alderwasley Park, owned by the Hurt family and enclosed about the year 1715. It covers around one hundred and ninety-four acres and holds oak, sycamore, beech, silver birch and copper beech trees. Around 1892 it grazed a flock of thirty Faroe Island black sheep and a ninety-head herd of fallow deer. Alderwasley Hall over on the right is a Georgian house with wings added after that period. The Hall has since been converted to a school, and although Alderwasley is often described as a hamlet, a church, built in 1815, stands within the Hall grounds. You are walking a section of the hills dividing the Ecclesbourne and Derwent valleys. Your route now passes the war memorial on the right. Copper beeches are beginning to dominate the landscape.

The next gate now leads onto the lane and you need to continue right, noticing over the wall the pool formed by damming the Pendleton Brook. The Hall's old stable block stands to the left and the lodge and formal wrought-iron lodge-gates to the right. At the road junction, turn right, using the Whatstandwell sign as your guide. Keep to the right-hand side so that you are facing the oncoming traffic. A small herd of Hereford cattle can sometimes be seen around the stockyard and paddocks to your right, while over to your left stands the long-abandoned chapel which has some interesting features dating from the sixteenth century.

You now need to follow the road down while keeping an eye out for the traffic, especially on the bends. After passing New Road Farm, the road dips and bends noticeably. This is typical Derbyshire landscape; walled fields and quite prominent ash trees, with cottages and farmsteads nestling in the valleys. Eventually you will reach the main roads (B5035 and A6). Cut right over the grass, noticing the mill house set back along the track and young holly bushes making an entanglement of the hedgerow. The pavement is over to your left. Cross with care, then continue over the Derwent and Railway Bridge to the Derwent Arms, just uphill from which is the Cromford Canal.

If you have parked back at Cromford, then another walk along that interesting canal stretch awaits you. If you are starting back from here, a pedometer would inform you that on the second section of the canal, Shining Cliff Wood, and Alderwasley up to this point you have covered a distance of $7^{1}/_{10}$ miles. It took me 3 hours and 40 minutes and I took thirteen thousand, six hundred and fifty-five steps!

Cromford

The inventive and highly successful Sir Richard Arkwright here, in 1771, built the first cotton mill to be fed by local streams. This splendid village nestling within a fortress of rock scenery, today attracts fly fishermen, rock climbers, abseilers, walkers, historians and sightseers from many parts of the British Isles. Arkwright, having built the village, utilised not only the millstreams but also the idea of mass production. Cromford formed a living blueprint for the first factory and Arkwright's mill attracts many visitors. The Dam, Scarthin Bookshop, and the Via Gellia, a ravine of two miles, are all worth visiting, along with the fifteenth century bridge spanning the Derwent.

High Peak Railway

Many engineers and enthusiasts regarded this enterprise as unique. Built nearly one hundred and seventy years ago, the line was designed to connect the Cromford Canal with the Peak Forest Canal at Whaley Bridge. The steepest gradient of 1 in $8^{1}/_{2}$ occurred near the Cromford termination point. The total length was thirty-three miles. The route is now an established trail for both walkers and horse riders.

Willersley Castle

Situated within walking distance of Cromford Wharf, Sir Richard

Arkwright's planned mansion was designed by William Thomas. Building began in 1788 but three years later a fire destroyed some of the exterior and interior structures. Sir Richard was destined never to live there, as he died before its completion in 1792.

Lea Hurst — Home of Florence Nightingale

Florence Nightingale was born in Italy and named after the famous city. The second daughter of Edward William Shore, she learned that her father had been left, among other things, a fine country estate centred around Lea Hurst, a seventeenth century farmhouse. Shore changed his name by deed poll to Nightingale. He was also approached by Sir Richard Arkwright to whom he sold, for twenty thousand pounds, land on which Arkwright could build his long-desired Willersley Castle.

In 1858 Florence returned to Lea, where, for many years, she wrote articles and books on hospital management and nursing. After her death in August 1910, the house remained as Nightingale property until 1940, when it was sold by auction and became, in 1951, a residence donated to the services of the Royal Surgical Aid Society.

Information on the Cromford Canal

The history of the Cromford Canal has been well documented, collated and first published by the Cromford Canal Society Ltd in 1983. A worthy addition to any canal enthusiast's library, the booklet's title is *The Cromford Canal.*

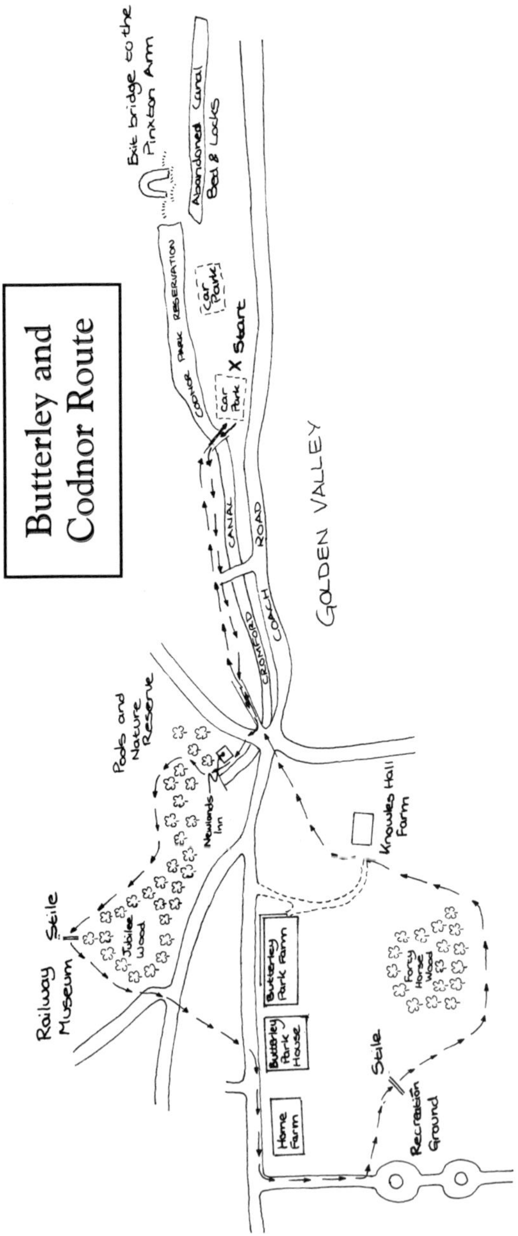
Butterley and Codnor Route
Exit bridge to the Pinxton Arm
Abandoned Canal Bed & Locks
Codnor Park Reservation
Car Park
Car Park
X Start
Canal
Cromford
Coach
Road
Golden Valley
Pools and Nature Reserve
Newlands Inn
Knowles Hall Farm
Stile
Railway Museum
Jubilee Wood
Butterley Park Farm
Butterley Park House
Forty Horse Wood
Home Farm
Stile
Recreation Ground

Exploring Codnor and Butterley

M1 Junction:	26 or 27, linking up with A608 or A610
Map Reference:	OS Pathfinder 795 SK 44/55
Start:	Coach Road, beside Codnor Park Reservoir
Car Parking:	Preferably the car park closest to the metal bridge
Buses:	From Victoria Centre, Nottingham — R1 Codnor, and Ironville From Derby, H1 to Codnor, hourly. Mon to Sat only or phone "Bus Line" (0113) 292200
Refreshments:	The Newlands Inn
Distance:	Approx 4 miles
Duration:	2 hours steady walking

About the walk

Stout footwear may be needed in the autumn and winter but you can usually get by with lightweight shoes or boots during a summer dry spell.

Beginning at Codnor Park Reservoir, the route follows the path of the Cromford Canal then continues through scrubland and a managed nature reserve, still connected to the waterway's original route. After passing the Midland Railway Centre and crossing a field or two, the road takes you for a short distance over a ridge. Then, by contrast, the route winds along a disused railway track before swinging across Golden Valley to complete this circular walk, which is easy and has variety.

The Route

On leaving the metal bridge, turn left onto the Cromford Canal towpath. Usually a pair of coot will be feeding in the same reedy area as the pair of mute swans. This pair, belying their name, communicate with each other and their cygnets by giving out a series of trumpet notes, particularly when the cygnets are just a few days old.

Ash, young oak, alder and elder thickets grow profusely on both sides of the canal. Notice the row of splendid stone cottages set back within the traditional-type gardens and with garden 'escapees' mingling colourfully among the wild flowers. Most of these cottages are renovated and were built by the Butterley Company in the 1790s. In the canal shallows, often close to the bank, you will see the shoals of minnows and sticklebacks and, around the reed stems, watersnails. In June, damsel flies will be on the wing and the dragonflies a month or so later.

On the first bridge, the company name, *Dorman Love, Middlesex* is engraved. I am told that at one time this was one of the largest bridge construction firms in the country. The canal bed, as you can see, becomes reedy in parts. You may disturb small birds like the wren, dunnock, robin, pied wagtail and blue tit from their forays along and around the wall niches to your right. In June and July there are stands of wild rose. From April to August you will see the green-veined white — a butterfly species largely reliant on garlic mustard and other wild growing plants of the cabbage family.

Valley Hall House, on the right, resembles, at first glance, a mill. A four-storey building, it was originally built by the Butterley Company and later became the Old Codnor Park and Ironville Co-op. In recent years, however, it has been converted into flats. At the bridge, proceed up to the road and the Newlands Inn opposite. You need to cross here and take the narrow walk in front of the pub to get on to the next section of canal towpath. The ash trees are mature along this stretch, and hawthorn, umbellifers and ground ivy also proliferate. Eventually you will reach the Butterley Tunnel which was narrow and took narrowboats with beams extending to around seven feet. For some transportation companies, the tunnel proved inadequate, as did the shallow canal reach associated with it.

You need now to retrace your steps from the Butterley Tunnel to the main road. On reaching the bridge, turn left and along by the front of the Newlands Inn to the car park.

On the pub wall to your left is a sign directing visitors to the *"Beer Garden and Children's Playground"*. Ahead is a chippings path. Use this and at the stile bearing the notice *"Country park, footpath to canal basin and golden valley light railway station only"* turn right and go over the stile with the railway to your left.

Continue along the wide path leading to the banks. These originated from coal dumps having become colonised by fast regenerating shrubs and trees like the silver birch, bramble and sycamore.

Use the railed wooden steps and at the top bear left to continue along the bank. Where the paths divide the easiest route is the one on the left from which you can glimpse the reeded remains of the Cromford Canal between the thickets.

Continue over the wooden bridge which takes surplus water from the banks down to the canal bed. Ignore the next set of steps cut into the banks and use the path centralised by a tree.

Swallows hawk for flies here in summer. Willow warbler, blackcap, chiffchaff, whitethroat and lesser whitethroat can be seen and heard along with resident species like bull, gold and greenfinch. The whinchat also passes through. This is scrubby, haw and elder habitat with reedy pools which, I suspect, were once the open 'flashes' that I saw in my boyhood from the windows of a Manchester-bound train. The area today is managed as a nature reserve with some interesting stands of reed and bulrush among the various willows.

The paths divide, but either one leads to the same place. One of the aquatic mammal species hereabouts is in the habit of leaving its droppings on a floating cross-rail of vandalised fencing. I would like to think that at least one pair of water voles are in residence, although it is more likely to be brown rats. The paths here are surfaced with limestone chippings. In June, notice the beds of birdsfoot trefoil (or 'eggs and bacon' as this plant is known locally). Daytime flying moths are common, not least of which is the six-spot burnet, which favours the trefoil and clover beds for laying its eggs, thus introducing the caterpillars to their respective food plants. Among the hawthorn you may see small ermine moths, cinnabar where groundsel or ragwort are growing, and a host of others.

Eventually, you will arrive at a rounded fence or stile with the compound of Brittain Pit on your right and Jubilee Wood, as the area of ash and hawthorn is known, to your left. Walk this path, noting the small stand of silver birch to your right. The path crosses the railway line. The pit headstocks and winding house are worth studying for the brickwork. The compound also serves as a smallholding where ducks, geese and a few pigs may be seen. If you look back across the fields, you can pick out the Swanwick Conference Centre and, off to its right, the buildings of the Hilltop Mink Farm. The compound fence turns, and you follow it. You need to turn again with the museum buildings of the Midland Railway Centre on your right.

This worthwhile project occupies some fifty-seven acres. Turn left down the track between the railway lines then locate a narrow path opposite, mostly overgrown around the fence sides, especially in June. If you have a dog, then now is the time to leash it, because the next stile will take you into a field usually grazed by Friesian youngstock.

Keep the hedge to your left, climb the tubular gate, then turn right and continue along the lane. Wildlife enthusiasts mention the fine dog-fox which crosses the field to forage around the bins of the Railway Centre, and the tawny owl pair that in summer evenings can be seen hunting for prey. Little owl, sparrowhawk and kestrel also hunt across these fields. Ahead, on a clear day, you should see Crich Stand again, marking its landscape link with the route of the Cromford Canal. The countryside opens up here. The Derbyshire town of Ripley is on the skyline to your left. Home Farm dominates in the fields to your left and below.

You will begin to meet up with traffic here, so take care. Turn left with Butterley Hall, now the modernised complex of the Derbyshire Police Headquarters, on your right. When you have passed the Butterley House Home for the Elderly enjoy the view down Golden Valley. Although the monument to canal engineer, William Jessop, rises above the trees, this is situated on private land with no current right of way.

Continue walking until you are level with the traffic island and keep this to your right. Within the arable fields, look for the recreation ground on your left. There is a hedge gap here. Go through it and bear left, keeping the hedge on your left. The bird most likely to be seen is the mistle-thrush but linnets, fieldfare and redwing will feed across the turf and hedgerows during the winter. Top the stile and proceed along the well-made path, winding through the elder and hawthorn thickets. Friends insist that this is locally known as Forty Horse Wood, an interesting name but hardly the mature tract of woodland I would have expected when I studied the map.

After what seems a fair walk you will reach a division of tracks. Take the one bearing left, and progress along another long path crossing the fields. When you are on the lane connecting Butterley Park Farm and Knowles Hall Farm, turn right. On the left, a footpath continues around a green tract, after which you need to swing left and, at the crossroads, walk on the right, over the bridge, and rejoin the towpath of the Cromford Canal. If you are in need of refreshment, The Newlands Inn is across the road. The canal towpath, or a section of the road called Golden Valley and an eventual right turn onto it, will then take you back to the Codnor Park Reservoir's metal bridge and car park.

Landlocked bridge at the Ironville end of Codnor Park Reservoir

Before leaving Codnor Park, if you have the time, spend a few minutes on the metal bridge. This stretch of water beside the car park was built as a water storage source for the Cromford Canal as was the nearby Butterley Reservoir. On both sides of this metal bridge, sizeable reed beds attract coot, moorhen, mallard, great crested grebe, reed buntings and pied wagtails. The swan pair currently resident nest in the reservoir reeds, then escort their cygnets across the car park and on to the canal soon after they have hatched, the shallower canal providing the surface weed on which the cygnets feed. When they are about two months old, however, and can root for different types of weed beneath the water surface, the cygnets are led back to the reservoir. Looking at the canal reed beds in the summer, you will see reedy mounds, or 'preening places', built up by the swan pair, and on which the family sleep and preen.

A local resident in his mid-fifties told me that a swan pair have nested here every year for as long as he can remember but the current pair began breeding in April 1996. Their bill colourations suggest that the pair are mature, and have probably bred elsewhere previously, or have paired after each losing a partner. The female, or 'pen', carries the number V26 on the yellow-banded leg ring. Known as a 'Darvic ring' the name is associated with the founder of this form of swan ringing and the yellow colouration also tells us that the swan was caught for ringing in Nottinghamshire.

From the reservoir car park you can follow the path beside the water, across the surface of which a family of great crested grebe can usually be seen. Notice the length and gauge of the nearby disused lock gates and stone bridge, landlocked now but once needed because the locally-termed 'Pinxton arm' of the canal met with the Ironville stretch here.

A brief history of the Butterley Company Works

This site can be seen on the left where the road dips below the Derbyshire Police Headquarters, a section of which was once the original Butterley Hall. Close by is Butterley Reservoir. This was built as a storage unit for the Cromford Canal. Neither of these sites is open to the public.

The Butterley Company Works was founded in 1790 by four men — Berresford, Outram, Jessop and Wright. In 1814, the year in which seventy-year-old William Jessop died, the company earned due recognition for having supplied the ironwork required for building the Vauxhall Bridge, which spans the River Thames. Butterley iron was also blended into the constructional workings of Scotland's Caledonian Canal.

Jessop's Monument

At the time of writing, Jessop's Monument is enclosed on a private tract of land but can be seen towering above the trees, especially if you have left Riddings and are walking down Bullock Lane to Ironville. However, in mid-July, the local history society sometimes stage a fine and informative exhibition in the Casson Street Church Hall. On first visiting this well-attended event in 1993, I discovered that minibus trips had been arranged to view the monument, which was opened with the landowner's permission. There we were met by a knowledgeable local historian, who told us that the seventy feet high monument was built with stone taken from the local gritstone quarries in 1854. It was financed, we were told, by money taken from the wage packet of each company employee!

Inside are one hundred and fifty spiral steps, and a plaque bearing the words 'Built by the workmen and friends of the late William Jessop of Butterley Hall as a tribute to his private work, great talents and public excellence'. The William Jessop in this instance was the son of the co-founder and, in later years, the term 'financed by public subscription' was used to explain how the costs of the monument's construction were met. Within living memory, the residents of Codnor and Ironville have trooped up to the monument, despite there having been many protesters. Plans seem to be afoot to re-open the site.

Golden Valley

This name describes the wealth to be found below ground — iron, coal and lime. The canals transported these from local kilns and provided a lucrative trade for a number of years.

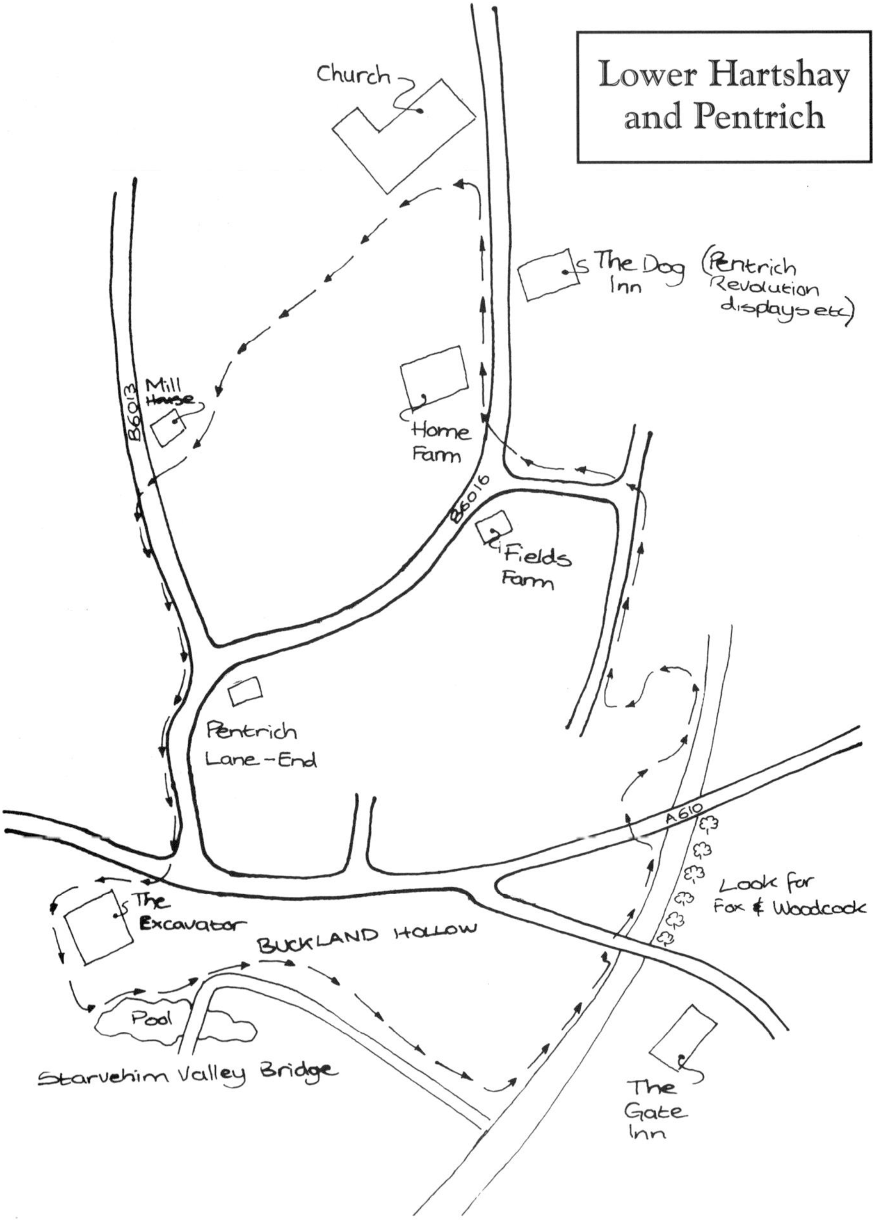
Lower Hartshay and Pentrich
Church
The Dog Inn (Pentrich Revolution displays etc)
Mill House
B6013
Home Farm
B6016
Fields Farm
Pentrich Lane-End
A610
Look for Fox & Woodcock
The Excavator
BUCKLAND HOLLOW
Pool
Starvehim Valley Bridge
The Gate Inn

Around Lower Hartshay and Pentrich

M1 Junction:	28 for the A38
Map Reference:	OS Pathfinder, Matlock (South) Sheet SK 25/35
Start:	Canal bridge near the Gate Inn, Main Road, Lower Hartshay
Car Parking:	As above
Buses:	From Derby — 123, 124 (study timetable) to Lower Ripley, no Sunday service From Ripley to Pentrich — Doyles bus 147 only Nottingham walkers — direct to Derby then 123, 124 Phone Bus Line (01332) 292200
Refreshments:	The Gate Inn, Lower Hartshay The Dog Inn, Pentrich The Excavator, Ripley Road
Distance:	$5\frac{1}{4}$ miles
Duration:	$2\frac{1}{2}$ hours

About the walk

This circular walk enables you to explore the Cromford canal towpath and the splendid little village of Pentrich before crossing the fields and taking in a wide and varied landscape, and returning to the canal.

One unavoidable nuisance is the A610, which you need to cross carefully, close to the beginning of the walk. Near the walk's end there is another crossing on Ripley Road, to reach the forecourt of The Excavator. There are no further main roads until you reach The Gate Inn. Stout footwear needs to be worn, since the field grasses hold moisture and the canal towpath is muddy in places. This aside, I have found that this route can provide a really interesting two and a half hours.

The Route

Having parked in the vicinity of The Gate Inn or the Cromford Canal Bridge, take the path down onto the towpath, then turn left and go under the bridge. The usual hawthorns, oaks and elders are in abundance. A man in a Ripley pub told me how he used to come down here to look for grass snakes, either coiled in the vegetation or swimming in search of minnows and small frogs.

Much of the canal bed now comprises reed and sedge, but it is still potentially good grass snake habitat. The present canal sides have been laid and made from blocks of precast concrete. To the left is a private residence and usually there will be a friendly 'good morning' if a member of the family happens to be in the garden.

The canal widens, and reeds and nettles are in evidence along with grass-bruised trails made by foxes. After climbing the stile at the end, climb the embankment steps, noticing the bramble thickets and blackberry harvest while bearing in mind the proximity of the A610 which you meet where the steps end. This road and its barriers cannot be rushed. It is a fast stretch of the road! Opposite, another flight of steps leads down the embankment — if you can locate them among the vegetation. If this is not possible, walk down to the track end, turn right and follow this down into the little valley, with a maze of fox paths in the grasses to your right. Down near the tubular gate, to the right, is a quite extensive and magnificent stand of teasel, those long-stemmed golden-headed plants attracting 'charms' of goldfinches and other small birds.

Turn right onto a grass track here and follow it a short way towards the embankment, while negotiating the nettles. Turn left at the stile. Go over it and venture for a few yards into the little wooded tract via another set of steps. You will find yourself on the canal towpath again. There is overhanging foliage here, mainly sycamore, hawthorn and some oak branches. On the opposite side, an old drain still releases water down to the canal bed.

Pink campion flowers are to be seen along here in early September. Notice the prolific carpets of ground ivy. Wide paths slope down to the towpath, then to the shallow bay below — a badger track or 'trod'. Oaks become more pronounced. The clatter of wood-pigeon wings breaks the sometimes prolonged silence. With so much screening vegetation around, this is an excellent place for watching wildlife. You are likely to come across a cluster of creamish-white objects in the towpath grasses. These are fox scats, usually tapering at one end. In the autumn they may be darker, due to the fox having fed on blackberries, elderberries and slugs. The pale bone-coloured scats contain just that substance — fragments of bone. In the reeds below the towpath sill, the fox paths continue and, on the opposite bank, notice the terracing paths beneath the oaks and elders and around the bracken fronds. One early September morning, I disturbed two young foxes here. One took refuge in the thicket to the left but the other, yellowish-brown and with a white-tipped brush, made off up the bank, then swung left along the terracing and screened itself in line with its litter companion.

Ground ivy and nettles are plentiful here. Peer into the pools but I doubt whether you will see any minnow or stickleback shoals. Some of the ash branches form a bower on the towpath. Under the rail-type bridge the pools widen. You could flush wild mallard here and a 'spring' of teal. Also notice the water forget-me-not. Notice the canal lengthmen's derelict bothie, partially covered with ivy. Ahead is a tunnel with a grid, and above it the A38. What you are looking for now is the path which goes off to your left, through the thickets and undergrowth, doubling back on yourself, but on higher ground. Ground ivy covers sections of brickwork here. Eventually you will find yourself on a grassy side with the Hartshay Brook chuckling away to your right.

When you are on the sandpath lane, turn right via a battered tubular gate and proceed along the wide track. Usually the hawthorn hedges are trimmed, but containing so few different plant species that they must have been planted in recent times. A plantation of silver birches should be on your left at first, then hedges on either side. When you reach a division of tracks, turn left, with Home Farm on the right in front of you. Walk the drive marked 'private drive' for a few yards only. A stile and footpath to your right diverts walkers away from the farm and up the field edge, with the hedge to your left. Take care if you have a dog with you because sheep occasionally graze this field and, beyond them, notice the hillock to the right. A sizeable rabbit warren!

Continue upfield by the farm until you reach a post and rail gate. Go over the stile to your left, and turn right. But be careful — this is a road used by traffic. There are neatly trimmed hawthorn hedge and bracken banks, then cottage fronts with splendid flower displays. A sign outside the stable facing the farmyard on the left usually informs the passerby that there are '*Pullet Eggs for Sale*'. You are now in Pentrich, famed for its 1817 revolution, about which I have included a few paragraphs at the end of this walk.

Here are some very fine and individual modern properties, blending admirably with historic ones. In a recess to the left stands an old pump, and on the right, The Dog Inn. Overlooking the pub car park is an artist's impression of Jeremiah Brandreth, one of the main personalities involved in the revolution.

By the steps of the church, to your left, you will see a footpath sign, indicating the walk across the fields to Mill House. This is the path you need to be walking, so climb the steps, noting the size variations in the flagstones at your feet. The church of St. Matthew looks splendid when seen in the morning light. The square, turreted tower signifies the Norman influence involved in its original structure, but restorations have taken place over the centuries. There are some old gravestones, one of which was erected in 1763.

The path narrows, and opposite the church porch a bruised grass track threads between the gravestones. Continue along this to the wall's slender gap stile. Carry on across the field towards the pylon and progress with the hedge on your right. Once you have topped the rise, the landscape opens up and, over to the right, you can pick out Crich Stand. The path now goes down to the tubular gate, after which you need to turn left and walk with the hedgerow to your left. Enjoy the view — the industrial sprawl of the Bull Bridge area dwarfed by the hills, valleys and woods into which the distant Lodge Hill Farm nestles. Down to the left is the edge of the Wingfield Park estate which extends across the landscape to Wingfield Manor near Alfreton.

The next stile is broader than those you have negotiated on your way across here. Having climbed it, again keep alongside the left hedgerow and notice how this field sits lower than the one to your left. Follow the curving field boundary round, until you are walking downhill. The contours then take you slightly uphill, and on your right is Mill Cottage. Children or dogs running ahead need to be called back, because you are approaching a surprisingly busy section of road. Go over the stile, keeping an eye on the traffic, and cross when you can turn left.

This is part of the Amber Valley, and the watercourse of that name threads across the fields a few yards away while keeping well out of sight. Not too far down the road you will pass buildings which look to me every inch a homestead — Amberside Farm. The trees around the entrance

The often overlooked sign displayed outside The Dog Inn, Pentrich, depicting a character involved in the ill-fated revolution

gates are cypresses, wellingtonia, horse chestnut and turkey oak. Coming into the scene on the left now are Pentrich Lane End and the Devonshire Arms. The parish boundary stone is by the fence just to your right.

Continue by the low wall on your right and towards the busy road and T-junction. On the right is a lovely old lodgehouse beside the private access road to Wingfield Hall Farm and beyond. At the T-junction turn right, then, when you are by the cottage and opposite The Excavator, cross with extreme care. The Excavator is a spacious pub with a friendly staff. It is so-called because an actual excavator was once positioned on a bay section of the roof, but had to be removed when cracks began to appear in the ceiling. The building was originally called Ladybank House. It was built to serve the commercial purposes of the nearby Cromford Canal. There are several framed photographs of past narrowboat families displayed alongside an etching of Sir Richard Arkwright. There are also submission and apology notices from wrongdoers of that time, applying to the same stretch of canal.

On leaving The Excavator, you need to follow the car park round so that the pub is on your left and a railway bridge is ahead of you. Go under the railway bridge and, after you have passed the private residence on your right, notice the woodland enshrouding the railway line on this same level. This is called Buckland Hollow. Notice the old pastureland coming down from the skyline ridge, across which runs the Roman-laid Ryknild Street. If you look on the map you will see Coneygrey Farm nearby, which was also a Roman garrison-type settlement.

Turn left when you reach the pool which, I am told, has been developed from the original canal bed. If you have the pool to your left then cross the end of it so that the water is to your right and the hedgerow to your left. You are now on the canal towpath, with a fox path in both the grasses and reeds. As you come round the bend you will not miss the old hump-backed Starvehim Valley bridge. Ahead, the path continues along the hedgeside to the farm at the far end, then it's just a matter of connecting up with the old canal bed again.

As an alternative, you can swing left out of the bridge path, turn right and go along the green lane, with a farm on the right. Ahead is a broad gravel track and low barbed wire fence, with a hawthorn hedgerow to the right. Turn right and meet the curve of pavement, then pass, (or call in to) the George Inn on the left. Turn right again down Bridle Lane by walled fields, and with the pool in the field on your left. After the last of the cottages on the left you will arrive again at the canal bed, so climb the stile and progress along the towpath. Notice the nine or ten renovated cottages on the opposite bank. They may be pre-Victorian and once associated with the canal and Bridge End Farm, which is also attached to the little settlement.

Willow trees as well as reeds and sedges are taking over the canal bed here. There are also stands of silver birch and alder. In the marshy tract to the left, look out for the occasional heron and 'wisp' of snipe. By September the red berries of the wild arum (or 'lords and ladies') should be burning through the hedge bottom. Where the bank sweeps down from the waters edge various aquatic weeds have colonised the pools.

At the canal bridge the circuit ends, unless you are thirsty. The Gate Inn is another welcoming hostelry and one wonders if the original buildings were associated with a coaching inn, and the nearby road a toll road. Like many pubs, however, it may have originally been a farmhouse. The landlady told me that the main structure of the building as we know it today was completed in 1834 and the premises opened as an inn.

Around Ripley

As a boy, leaning on the low wall and sipping lemonade in front of the Three Ponds public house at Nuthall, I used to study each blue and white liveried Midland General bus when it came by, and wonder not only at the destinations but how the place names came about. Watnall, Codnor, Ripley? How did towns and villages come by such names.

Later, I learned that Ripley is a name associated with the Anglo Saxons, and probably signified the whereabouts of a settlement clearing used for both trading and growing crops. The Domesday reference shows it spelt as 'Ripelie' and one wonders if this referred to the crops, as opposed to the actual settlement. Coneygrey Farm, which I mentioned earlier, is associated with a small Roman garrison and the locally famous road, Ryknild Street, passes nearby.

The Charters of Darley Abbey contain interesting paragraphs of medieval and Norman history, and references are made around 1250-51 to the Abbot of Darley's request, granted by Henry III, to hold an annual fair and weekly market in the town centre. The Abbot was host to Henry III at that time, the royal presence being connected to a bout of hunting taking place in and around Duffield Forest. I wonder if the name Buckfast Hollow also originated at or around that time.

Ripley was locally very much to the fore throughout the industrial revolution; being surrounded by iron belts and coalfields. Benjamin Outram founded the Butterley Company in 1792 as there was a wealth of minerals still to be extracted. 'The Outram Way', an early form of colliery railway track, connected Ripley to a canal wharf at Little Eaton and the Cromford Canal began its role in commercial transportation in 1793, lasting at least until the railway superseded it in 1856. Ripley was by then a town which attracted people from the surrounding villages, just as it does today. The Ripley Co-operative Society was formed in 1860. The original village green was situated where the Market Place stands today, overlooked by the Town Hall, which, when built in 1880, was known as the Market Hall.

In the mid 1970s commercial traffic was so heavy, keeping the residents awake at night as lorries and freightliners negotiated the steep hills, that bypass roads were deemed necessary and plans to lay them were soon underway. If you are walking the shopping streets you will come across views over the Derwent and Amber valleys. The Peak District foothills are only a short distance away.

The Pentrich Revolution

The Derbyshire village of Pentrich is associated with a group of revolutionaries who, in June 1817, set out for Nottingham and were seen as terrorists on foot. Jeremiah Brandreth and two other men led this march, which was intercepted by a troop of Hussars from which his supporters fled, while Brandreth, determined to stand his ground, was arrested along with a further twenty or so who were jailed or transported. Brandreth and his two accomplices were hanged and beheaded.

Recommended reading:

A really well-researched account of the Pentrich Revolution was completed by John Stevens in 1977. Entitled *England's Last Revolution*, it was published by the Moorland Publishing Company and is a unique and detailed record of the revolution, which was short-lived. Severe examples were made of its perpetrators.

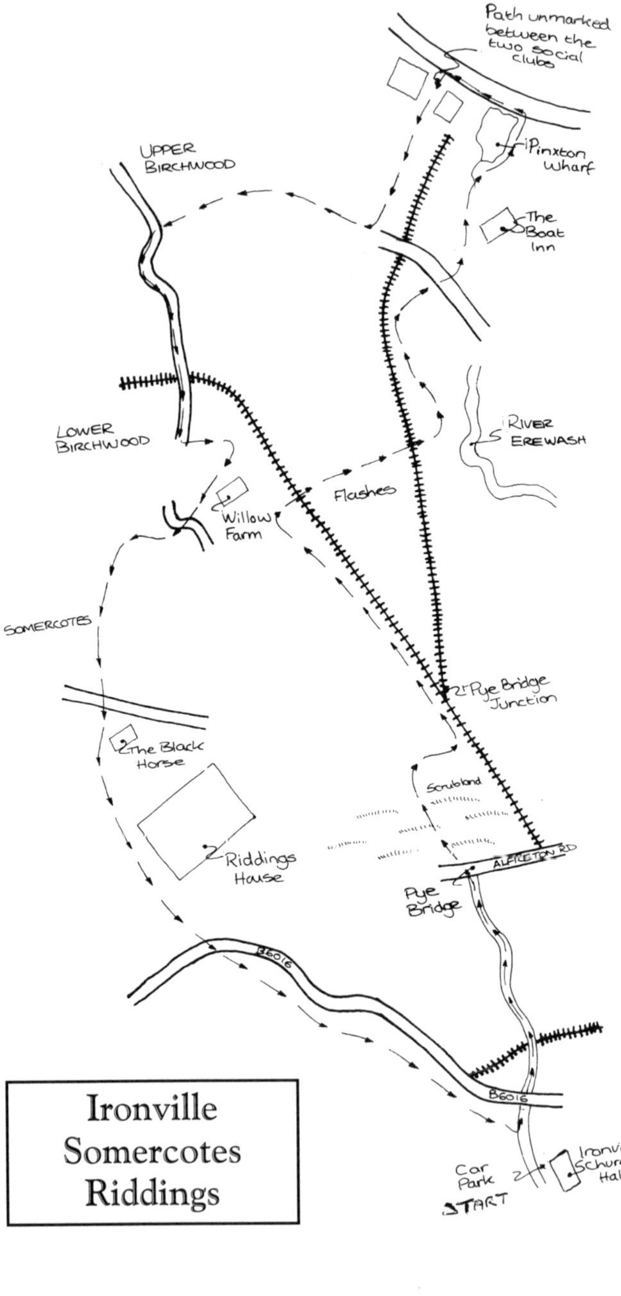

Ironville Somercotes Riddings

Ironville–Pinxton–Somercotes–Riddings An Eight Mile Circular

M1 Junction:	26 or 27 linking up with A608 or A610 (Eastwood/Codnor)
Map Reference:	OS Pathfinder 795 SK 44/55
Start:	The Church Hall, Casson Street, Ironville
Car Parking:	Behind the Church Hall
Buses:	From Victoria Centre, Nottingham — R1 Codnor, and Ironville From Derby — H1 Codnor
Refreshments:	The Boat Inn, Pinxton Wharf The Black Horse, Somercotes The New Inn, Riddings
Distance:	8 miles
Duration:	3½-4 hours

About The Walk

This route can become heavily waterlogged, especially around the land reclamation and opencast sites. I have, in late August, worn wellingtons and been glad I did so, especially around Pinxton. Somercotes and Riddings, however, are comparatively easy and normally water-free routes.

Be careful on the stretch of busy and winding road between Pinxton and Somercotes. You are walking downhill, the traffic coming up hill, often at speed. There is at least one blind bend along here, so listen for the traffic as well as looking!

The rest of the walk is worth the risk, as a pleasant hedgeside walk over the fields stretches ahead, the regulars at The Black Horse Somercotes are friendly and you will pass several green corners on the path through Riddings. After that it is literally downhill all the way to your Ironville starting point.

The Route

From the car park behind the church hall, you need to make for the nearby Bullock Lane bridge.

Lime and sycamores, hedgerows of elder and hawthorn provide the greenery, and as you turn with the bend and the housing blocks in sight, there is a stand of horse chestnuts to your left.

The nettle beds attract small tortoiseshell butterflies and you will also see peacock, orange tip and red admiral.

Beyond the railway bridge the elder thickets and scrubland become apparent. You may glimpse blackbird and dunnock. The robins along here are quite tame and probably roost in the outbuildings of the pony paddocks to your right.

Eventually you will reach the ruins of what appears to be a bridge and here, with care, you need to cross the road and continue along the path.

Burdock, thistles, various stages of oak, hazel, ash and rowan are quite prolific on either side, the hazel nuts being well formed by late August.

The stands of alder and hazel on the right screen the sewage works. You may disturb small flocks or 'charms' of goldfinches and the entire habitat is an obvious haven for small, frequently unseen mammals like the field vole and long tailed fieldmouse, which are hunted by the stoat and weasels. One weasel I disturbed here bounded high above the grass tufts before disappearing into the low undergrowth.

The hazel and willow become thick hereabouts and eventually, over to the left, you will see a small pond, probably formed from residue water, which holds at least one breeding pair of moorhens.

At the next bridge take the steps to your right, then bear left and across. By the notice *Main Road* and the last house in the row, you will see a footpath sign, and here you need to turn right.

Again the path takes you through scrubland thicket and leaves the canal bed for some way. Although this is an extensive tract of land, keep the embankment on your left and where the path, or paths, allow, veer gradually to your right so that an opencast site and the railway are ahead.

The wildlife potential here is excellent, but with the exception of foxes it is essentially small bird and small mammal country with willow warblers, whitethroat and lesser whitethroat cocks singing from their territorial posts in the late spring and summer.

When you are close to the railway, the path bears now to the left. You will next see fields to your left and the railway to your right, and this is the route, by Pye Bridge Junction, you need to be following.

The fields are pleasantly undulating and are, I think, a mixture of old parkland and land reclaimed from previous opencast workings.

The grass and vegetation is usually long here and parted only by the occasional rambler.

Here and there, you will see paths in the undergrowth made by foxes, crossing to and from the fields. This boundary fence trail is longer than might be expected and you might wonder from time to time if you are on the right path. But keep going and notice as, you come to a small paddock-type orchard on your left, the height of the hawthorn trees. These are probably at the maximum height for the species.

Eventually, you will see the ruins of a barn and the foundations of buildings, perhaps cowsheds, in the nearside corner of the field. Then to your right you will see a railway tunnel. Go under this and continue down the wide gravel track, the rich grazing land to your left, the two tree and marshy tracts to your right.

These were once 'flash-pools' tenanted by itinerant and numerous mute swans, which also grazed the fields and were attracted down by the then close by Cromford Canal and River Erewash.

There is a second railway arch and ahead, an unscenic view of outcropping. Cross the plank bridge over the slender watercourse here, turn left and follow the path.

Over to your right, and currently lined and strengthened by limestome and chippings, probably due to the outcropping, runs the River Erewash, an aquatic boundary dividing Derbyshire and Nottinghamshire.

Magnesium limestone holds the water-course in check, but on its determined way down to the Trent both clay and shale provide channelings.

Up ahead you will see a works yard depot. Don't be put off, because at its boundary your path swings right. You are walking within sight of the Amber Valley boundary, still with the Erewash in sight, until you reach a stile, leading you across the hardstanding entrance of the works yard. You need to be bearing right to cross the main road.

Brace yourself, because here the road surface is usually hidden by layers of water, mud and coal slurry. Go carefully, while watching for the occasional car or lorry travelling the road.

Once across, having quietly cursed me I expect, the path by the narrow watercourse beckons. I promise you, the prospects ahead are more interesting.

This narrow strip of water is all that remains of the Cromford Canal hereabouts although the next few hundred yards also retains remnants of its history. Among the stands of reed, sedge and water forget-me-not you will see the leaves of the giant water dock. Pied wagtails and moorhens make use of this narrow stretch, which has become overgrown by reeds and vegetation. To the right is a grassy picnic area.

The white cottage ahead is The Boat Inn, a dwelling with an interesting history.

After a few more reeds and willows, Pinxton Wharf comes into view; a four or five acre stretch of water with grass sloping to the water's edge and a tree-clad island. Young anglers are encouraged here and there are picnic tables close by.

The current mute swan pair have been breeding here for several years and are not typical, because the elderly pen has a large rounded 'knob' or berry at the base of the bill and could be mistaken for the cob.

A local angler told me about the successive broods of seven to nine cygnets; a cob cygnet of this last brood being about the largest I have seen.

When you leave the Wharf, turn left and cross the bridge, then pass two social clubs. Although there is not at present a recognised footpath sign, according to the map a footpath does exist.

Bypass the cottages, go up the steps on the right and on to the footpath with the horse paddock over on your right. Continue between the elder and hawthorn thicket and notice the water, forming channels and finding its level as it leaves the reclaimed land.

This again can prove to be a wet and soggy stretch. You may disturb flocks of linnet, green and goldfinches from the thickets.

Keep the fence to your right and follow it round by the road. One path, leading from the field corner and bearing left, will invite you down to a reedy pool, then persuade you to climb back on to this route. Continue by the fence and following the field boundary, then when the fenceline ends, turn right into a splendid green lane.

Hawthorn is abundant and there are a few field boundary oaks. As you continue uphill, notice how the hawthorns have been intentionally planted or persuaded into a straight line. The foliage meets above you to form a tunnel, especially in late summer.

When you reach the ridgetop, continue along the boundary fence, which should be to your left and separating a road. Keep going for several hundred yards to a stile on the left, with a stile in the fence on the opposite side. Climb the stile and cross the road via the pedestrian crossing, then go over the next stile. The path is ahead. Follow the bruisings across the grass so that eventually you have a field corner and boundary hedge to your left, mostly comprising hawthorn and ash. Reach the double hedge and begin looking for a stile, which is difficult as branches almost overhang its position and you may well go past it.

Having climbed this stile, continue now with the hedgeline on your right. If you have children or dogs running ahead call them back, because the next stile ahead takes you on to the very busy stretch of road I mentioned earlier.

When you have climbed the stile, turn left and cross so that you are facing oncoming traffic. This is a fast road with bends, and has no pavement.

After four or five minutes walking, you will arrive at the railway bridge. Look on your left for the footpath sign and farmgate, by the side of which is a posting box marked *Babylon Farm*.

Go along this track until you reach another green lane between the hedgerows. Turn right, and follow this up between the Lower Birchwood farms, then turn left. Some of the buildings here are ornate. Enjoy the peaceful atmosphere, and in the summer take advantage of the shade created by the overhangs of ash foliage.

Time now, though, to look for the stile to the right. Climb it, then turn left and right, following the hedgeline to your right. This is a well-walked path across cattle pasture, until you reach the two steps and a stile. Climb these, and the hedgeline is now on your left and you are within the Somercotes boundary.

Another stile at the bottom end of the field has the remains of an old tree alongside. Beyond here, keep on the path with the fence to your right.

This is broken country — tracts of thicket and long grasses attract butterflies, moths, small mammals and birds, especially beyond the tubular gate to your right, where flattened grasses and paths suggest that a sizeable litter of fox cubs is being reared.

There are raspberry canes here, so, if not an orchard, this was probably once managed as allotments. The gravelly broken-surfaced road ahead and between the houses and bungalows, takes you up to the Somercotes main road.

Beyond the Black Horse turn immediate right and venture uphill a little way, between the bungalows. When you see two short concrete posts ahead, step by them and turn immediately left, so that the wall and a square of pleasant and private residences are on your left. The square or oblong arrangement of these buildings suggests that a sizeable farm was once established here.

Continue along a narrow wooded lane which bears directly alongside parklands, with sizeable, fenced paddocks and small woods to your right.

To your left is an estate lodgegate house, then the walled Hall overlooked by chestnut trees, and on the right, Park Mews, again private residences, but once serving no doubt as the country estate courtyards.

You are now in Riddings and at the lane end need to turn left. I was told by a member of the Codnor and Ironville Local History Society that the original place name denotes 'a clearing in the forest'!

This is Church Street. Notice the different types of homesteads as you follow the bending road and pass the thatch-roofed Moulders Arms on your right. Continue to Market Place which is a widened bend in the road, then up to the New Inn to the left. This is also a welcoming pub, where in nice weather you can sit outside.

When you leave this hostelry, turn left, and at the T-junction, left again. Just check here that you are walking the downhill route on Bullock Lane.

Eventually, as the lane bends, you will see Riddings Wood on the left beyond the hedgerow and a field's width away. But no footpath is definable and a little farther along, the pavement peters out. With care, cross to the right pavement, by Oak Cottage, after which the road slopes noticeably. Over on the opposite ridge, Jessops Monument strikes high above the trees.

When you are over the railway bridge notice how unclustered the graveyard to your right seems. In the summer the grass is closely mown and complemented by the yews and cypresses.

At the end of Bullock Lane, turn right, for here is the church hall, behind which your car should be parked, this circular walk having reached its completion. You have walked a little over 8 miles. It took me four hours and about fifteen thousand, five hundred steps!

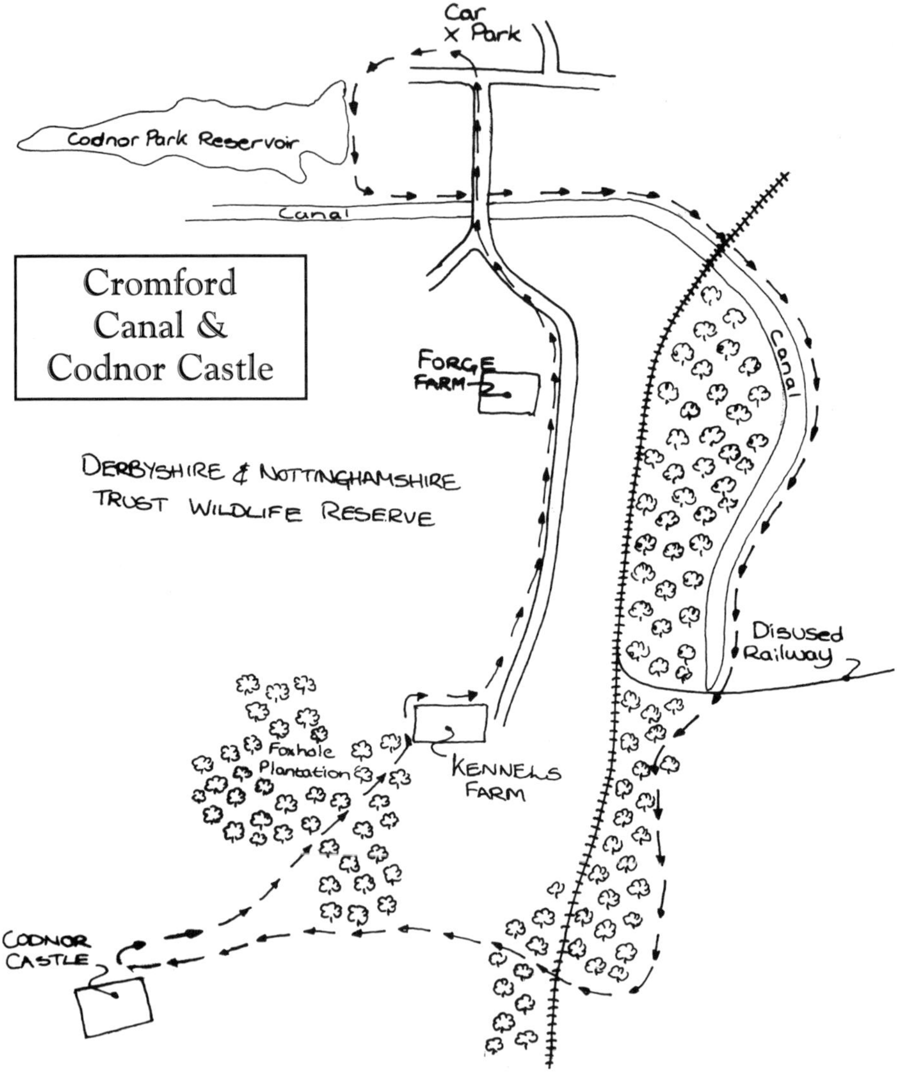
Car Park
Codnor Park Reservoir
Canal
Cromford Canal & Codnor Castle
FORGE FARM
DERBYSHIRE & NOTTINGHAMSHIRE TRUST WILDLIFE RESERVE
Canal
Disused Railway
Foxhole Plantation
KENNELS FARM
CODNOR CASTLE

Cromford Canal–Codnor Castle

Start: Cromford Canal

Distance: 3½ miles

Duration: 1½–2 hours

The Route

If you are parked behind Christ Church Hall, Ironville, begin the walk by following the path (originally an arm of the canal) with the church at your back.

The path goes beneath a low footbridge between willows, sycamores and by pony paddocks and allotments to the post-and-rail fenced edge of Codnor Park Reservoir. Keep the fence to your right, walk the width of the reservoir and bear left at the Pinxton Arm landlocked bridge.

The canal section should be to your right. Notice the width of the waterway and length of the locks. Keep to the towpath. One interesting building on the opposite bank was obviously a wharf, built as narrowboat loading and unloading premises. Some of the ruined wall-edges suggest there were several more such buildings.

One building served as lodgings for intinerate workers and was known as 'the dosshouse'. Another provided stabling for over one hundred horses.

Because we are close to houses and buildings, we have to contend with litter over the next five or six hundred yards. Alders fringe the canal course for a short distance. There are also willow trees and a few poplars.

Away to the left, Jacksdale nestles in a valley. Up ahead you will find an unsafe, fenced-off bridge, with the canal towpath continuing beyond it.

Here the canal swings noticeably with the River Erewash, winding through the fields and scrubland over to the left. The woodland on the opposite bank screens the foundations and ruins of industrialisation. As you continue along the path, it becomes difficult to think of industry, yet this area and Ironville, in particular, was considered once to have been the most industrialised place in Great Britain. Bracken flanks the towpath. Reed and sedge make every effort to hide the water.

This is a good place for reedbuntings, daylight flying moths and dragonflies.

Where the willow tangles overhang, look out for a kingfisher. If you are scanning through binoculars, you want the line of low branches rather than the high one. The kingfisher may well fly across to follow the course of the river upstream.

I would expect to see an occasional water-rail here too, especially in winter when titmice are passing through the woods in their search for food.

Small mammals thriving here, but usually remaining unseen, will be long tailed fieldmice and voles and their predators, the stoat and weasel. You can see rabbit digs and fox trails beneath the trees on the opposite side, but usually only when the ground cover has died away in midwinter.

When you reach an old railway bridge, cross the water by the stepping stones, then climb the stile on the left. This area is designated a nature reserve, managed by the Nottinghamshire and Derbyshire Wildlife Trusts.

Incidentally, if you look to the left as you are progressing along the fenceside, you will see how the base of the railway embankment was once reinforced with local stone.

To your left is a really fine wildlife habitat, but the list of potential species would take up several pages. A fair proportion of the birds, mammals, amphibians, plants, insects and butterflies you'll see mentioned in any book on wetland and meadow's edge thrive here, so disturbance should be kept to the minimum.

Back in the 1980s, a Langley Mill birdwatcher related how he had watched short-eared owl and marsh harrier quartering here. The summer which brought the Great White Egret into the Trent Valley also attracted several night herons. I saw one at a distance of forty feet in a pool on the nearby Langley Mill Flashes, and another was recorded here on the same evening.

The scrubland over to the right is the type of place to see a bullfinch or two. The summer-visiting warblers and butterflies find this a splendid habitat.

Moving on, you come to a rail and concrete fence just by a widespreading willow.

Turn right here and go over the stile. There are several paths, but you need to make your way steadily to the left and the railway bridge.

In January, you will notice how the coverts are hunted over by foxes. The pungent scent is always thick in the air. Notice the shoots and bark-stripping by the rabbits.

There are several small attractive pools, the type sought out by 'springs' of teal, but these duck will leave at the slightest disturbance.

When walking through habitat like this, two should be regarded as a crowd if you are hoping to see something of the birds and mammals. On crossing the railway bridge, you may be surprised by the width of the track. This is reminiscent of marshalling yards, which must have formed a busy scene in the early part of this century.

Another tract of scrub woodland needs to be passed through, then there is a field tract to be walked, to the side of Foxhole Planatation.

The ruins of Codnor Castle

The Amber Valley waymarker indicates that here the path continues inside, but along, the boundary of this wood. In line with the woodland corner the path sweeps upfield, towards the hilltop ruins of Codnor Castle. The land slopes over to your left here. Cattle are grazed on these fields. The farm alongside is a strictly private residence.

After the long but gentle haul up to the ruins, pause and take in the view around you. The woods of Moorgreen and Annesley rise on the far horizon, and on a clear day you can just about locate Bestwood on Nottingham's urban fringe. Jessop's Monument is of course, much closer, and prominent above the trees.

The ruins of Codnor Castle date back to the reign of Henry III and succeed an earlier fortress administered by William Peveril. A few further paragraphs on Codnor Castle are to be found at the end of this section. Leaving the castle, you need now to retrace your steps for a short distance, then gradually bear left to the stile that takes you into Foxhole Plantation. An early morning walker may flush a heron from the pool to the left.

This and other such ponds, while serving as drainage pools, may well have been designed or at least used as a duck decoy unit, in Victorian or Edwardian times.

The trees are basically beech and sycamore, but I think oak would have been prevalent in earlier years.

The ground is furrowed and hollowed. Ground ivy is prolific. To the right, as you walk the dividing path, are three trees, and a low ridge which appears to have been a boundary marker or where pheasant pens or the decoymen's hut were situated, perhaps less than a hundred years ago.

I love woods like this. The leaf and ground layer is thick, and attracts large inland waders like woodcock, which also feed around the margins of the Brinsley/Aldecar Flashes. You may see a tree creeper, nuthatch or greater spotted woodpecker or hear a coal-tit calling. It is an intriguing place.

When you come upslope to the field's edge you may see a sign advising you of the bull in the field ahead. However, you need only cross those few yards to the stile on your right. Climb this, and make your way down the hedgeline of Kennel's Farm on your right.

It's a downfield walk, with a lane coming in on your right and horse paddocks ahead. Strictly speaking, the footpath cuts across a corner of the paddock, but if you are nervous of horses and ponies I don't suppose anyone would mind if you climbed the fence to your right to reach the lane.

Either side are the paddocks, horses and three or four Shetland ponies. This is Forge Farm, and as you continue along the road, you will pass Forge Row and then Railway Row, with houses and bungalows of different styles on the left side.

Bear left and across the end of Monument Lane, then cross the canal bridge directly at Cinder Bank, which leads you by the green way on either side known as Market Place.

A few yards on, you will see the school on your right and Christ Church ahead, with the hall to your left and your car parked behind it.

Codnor Castle

William Peveril was first associated with Codnor's original fortress and here the Grey family built the castle with a two thousand acre park, in the reign of Henry III. It would have been an impressive building, moated, with a significant gateway, a drawbridge, two sizeable courtyards and four towers.

In present times you can feel the Norman influence, so it would do you little harm if you let your imagination run away with you for a few minutes, before taking in the ruins, portions of the towers, courtyard wall and dovecote. Much of the stonework from this castle has since been used in the building of various farms and cottages within walking distance of the site.

Behind the ruins stands Castle Farm which is still a working farm.

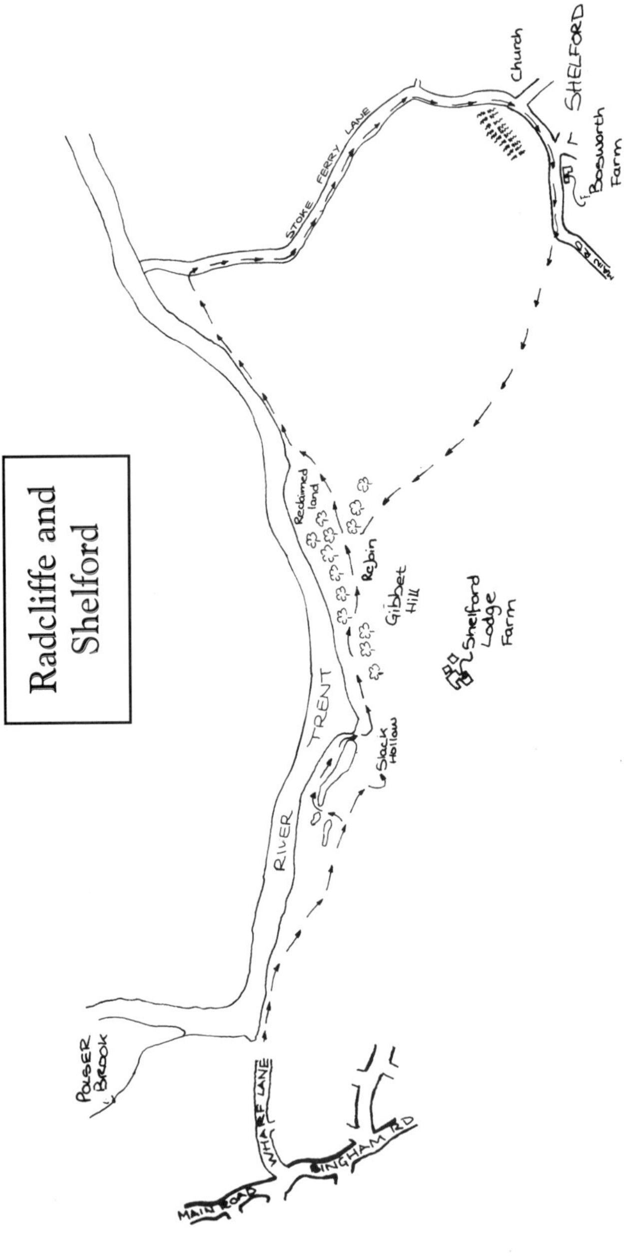
Radcliffe and Shelford
SHELFORD
Church
Bosworth Farm
MAIN RD
STOKE FERRY LANE
Reclaimed land
Gibbet Hill
Shelford Lodge Farm
RIVER TRENT
Slack Hollow
POLSER BROOK
WHARF LANE
MAIN ROAD

Radcliffe-on-Trent to Shelford

Map Reference:	OS Pathfinder 834 SK 63/73 and 813 SK 64/74
M1 Junction:	Junction 24 for A453 and A6110 or Lings Bar Road
Start:	Wharf Lane, Main Road, Radcliffe on Trent
Car Parking:	Where signs indicate
Buses:	From Broad Marsh or Market Street, Nottingham — L2, L3, L4
Refreshments:	The Manvers Arms, Radcliffe on Trent
Distance:	3½ miles
Duration:	About 1½ hours or 2 hours if exploring Slack Hollow

About The Walk

Stout shoes are needed in the autumn and winter. At Slack Hollow, care should be taken when negotiating the cliffside steps. The walk is easy-going and in the warmer months, leisure-type footwear is quite adequate.

The wildlife enthusiast will find his or her walk enhanced by binoculars. If you are interested in looking over ornamental gardens, you should put twenty minutes aside to enjoy the seasonal delights of the Cliff Gardens.

The Route

Leave the bus, or park in the vicinity of The Manvers Arms on the Main Road in Radcliffe on Trent. A few strides from the pub you will reach the corner of Wharf Lane, where the walk begins.

Wharf Lane has a children's playground on the left and a private residence, Radcliffe Lodge, on the right. You will see a set of steps on the right of the railway bridge. Climb these, past the ivy-covered trees and masses of cow parsley and related umbellifers; the mobile home park and the River Trent in the background.

The river bends here. Just beyond the mobile home park, the mouth of the Polser Brook provides shallows where redshank and heron wade, and wigeon gather to graze the winter field.

On the opposite side of the river the Netherfield Lagoons gleam, while the nearby retail and industrial parks are just hidden from view.

Seasonal notes on the wildlife of this area will be found in the section describing the Stoke to Netherfield walk.

On our walk today though, you will probably see such garden and woodland bird species as the chaffinch, greenfinch, robin, blackbird, song and mistle thrush and collared dove as well as titmice, wrens and dunnock. Nuthatch, green, lesser and greater spotted woodpeckers are occasional visitors.

From mid-March until late April look out for the warblers, chiffchaff, willow warbler, blackcap and spotted flycatcher.

At most times of the year, you will catch a whiff of fox, especially where the paths open up. The green verge on the right becomes shaded by copper beach and whitebeam, while on the left, laburnum contrasts with the many oaks and the occasional horse chestnut.

You will see on the right the gated entrance to the small but beautifully maintained Rockley Memorial Park.

Here, you can either continue, or look around the park and return to the route. Another choice of directions awaits almost opposite the park gates, for here you can descend the steps or again continue along the walk.

To explore Slack Hollow, descend the steps with care. There are oaks, limes, sycamores, and copper beech on either side. Near the small pool on the left, several rowan or mountain ash saplings have been planted.

You will soon arrive at a gate and fence gap, with a pylon and the river ahead. Take the path that swings right and you will draw level with the river on your left.

This is another good warbler area, and woodcock, snipe and redshank can sometimes be seen.

Hawthorn and umbellifers proliferate, and from April through to the middle of May you will hear the 'carr carr' calls of young rooks echoing from the few nests on the opposite side of the river.

Coot pairs nest among the low willow branches here, and a mute swan pair attempt to breed amongst the reed and willow scrub, fringing either one of those two attractive pools beneath the cliff contours to your right.

The current swan pair occasionally cross to the river and walk around the weir to the lower reach, where they become almost camouflaged by the white water.

These pools are, I think, all that remain locally to signify the Trent's original course. The willows are likely to attract a kingfisher, and the stand of reed-mace and bulrush at the weir end of the pool serve as windbreaks.

Keep to the right of the white rails, and take the path winding right and on up to The Walk. In damp or wet weather, this path can be precarious. You will soon find yourself among willow, hawthorn, sycamore and horse chestnut trees again.

In the autumn, various fungi including the honey fungus and shaggy ink cap appear.

Continue Along The Walk

When you have reached The Walk, turn left. Bypass the holly and chestnut trees and stands of pink blossoming hawthorn. At the green barrier the houses end, and the fields of Gibbet Hill slope and fold noticeably from the skyline. Estate gamekeepers probably used to display their strings of pest corpses or 'gibbets' here but today both the Gibbet and nearby Malkin Hill are arable land, and almost the only place where the sight of gabbling canada geese squadrons rising from the late summer stubble in the evening light seems to harmonise with the river valley scene. I am concerned that these birds are locally overpopulated and believe that their numbers should be kept to a manageable number.

You are now following the course of a floodbank, the scrubland to your left having been a sizeable, year-round, backwater known as Radcliffe Osiers, once hunted over by at least one pair of otters.

The last otter sighting for this section of the Trent Valley occurred around 1955. Green and golden plover still flock and feed on these river side fields throughout the winter and you may disturb snipe, redshank, woodcock and migratory green sandpipers.

The river will remain out of sight until you have topped the next stile, and continued for a few hundred yards. You might then see the herons and common terns.

On the opposite side is Stoke Bardolph. A non-breeding population of mute swans preen in the sandy shallows on both sides, and assemble to feed on bread thrown from the mooring ramp in front of the popular Ferry Inn. You may surprise a pair of oystercatchers, but the tufted and wigeon drake escorting the feral mallard are, I think, collection birds.

The floodbank continues across the field which ewes and lambs usually graze from March to June. When you have climbed the floodbank stile turn right and walk facing oncoming traffic, preferably in single file because although low hedged, the lane is narrow and winding.

There is a hedge of nettles on the left, then haw thickets gradually take over. These fields are usually arable or grazed by sheep. You will come to the mellowed brickworks of Shelford Church tower. Still keeping to the right, descend into the historic manoral hollow, noticing the individual styles of the properties on either side.

Next you will reach a footpath sign, pointing to Radcliffe-on-Trent. Turn right as the sign indicates, and walk between the cottages and the clumps of ragwort playing host to caterpillars.

Grass stems and poppies reach to knee height in summer, but if you are winter walking, you may see hare trails lightly patterning the darker soils of the ploughland.

Where the paths divide, continue along the one on the left, keeping the hedgeline to your right where snowberry, field poplar, ash and rowan have been planted. Where the path turns right as you enter the next field, you will probably disturb a few rabbits. Adults lift and fluff their white scuts as a departure sign to warn their warren companions.

Still keep the planting and the hedge to your right, and you will meet with the floodbank, along which you have walked with Radcliffe-on-Trent at your back.

You are now facing it and returning upfield to Cliff Walk. Retrace your steps to Wharf Lane.

In this field, in June and July, you may see among the ragwort and daisies, a stand or two of meadow cranesbill, with its distinctive blue flowers.

The ninety degree bend along the River Trent as seen from Cliff Walk, Radcliffe-on-Trent

The Rockley Memorial Park

This section of the cliff was originally owned by Nottingham Colwick Estates Ltd, who sold the land to Mr Lisle Rockley of Richmond Drive, Mapperley, Nottingham, along with Cliff Walk, which he rightly describes as 'a broad and pleasant promenade'.

When this sale of land had been secured Mr Rockley then donated it to Radcliffe-on-Trent, his birthplace, so that its inhabitants 'could enjoy the cliffs and access to their River Trent forever'.

The memorial park was eventually council-maintained but Mr Rockley took a great interest in it, and provided food and nesting boxes for the birds.

The park was officially opened to the public on Saturday October 15th 1927 and 'dedicated to the memory of the Men of Radcliffe-on-Trent who fell in the Great War 1914-18'.

This is still a beautifully maintained and colourful tract of land.

Brief Histories of...

...Radcliffe-on-Trent

Situated seven miles east of Nottingham, the original settlement and church of St. Mary was financially supported by Stephen de Radcliffe, who arrived soon after the Norman Conquest. Another family, the d'Ayncourts, also owned a substantial tract of land and remained until the fifteenth century, with Robert d'Ayncourt being recorded as St. Mary's second benefactor.

Throughout the Middle Ages, the population remained at about 100-150, most of whom were in some way connected with working the land.

In 1487, on 16th June, Henry VII attended two masses in Church before riding the short distance to the battlefield. That became locally known as The Red Dyke due to seven of the sixteen thousand assembled there losing their lives in what has long been termed 'the bloodiest battle ever waged on English soil' — the Battle of East Stoke.

Once the River Trent became linked with the locally important canal networks, Wharf Lane was used daily by coalcarts, assembling to meet the barges coming in from the Nottinghamshire and Derbyshire coalfields.

Coal was allocated in half or one hundred weight tons to the local people, including those residing in the Vale of Belvoir.

The return cargoes were of corn and cereal crops. Willows were grown as a crop for basket-making on what today is the mobile home site.

Near the village centre stand some fine properties built in Victorian and Edwardian times.

Although today modern estates and daily commuter travel contrast with the quiet village scene, Radcliffe is rightly regarded as a green-edged community linked to the second longest river in England, the Trent.

In 1926 some of the cottages were sold to townsfolk seeking a country retreat and in 1960 the previously unnamed streets received due recognition. Today, almost every corner of the village hosts a name plaque indicating the whereabouts of, for instance, Pinfold or Stoke Ferry Lane.

...Shelford

The Shelford Church of St. Peter and St. Paul is best known for its tower, which houses a clock and five bells.

The font is believed to be fourteenth century and the register dates from 1563.

In 1878, the church was completely restored by the Earl of Caernarfon, the cost having been eight thousand pounds. Monuments to the Stanhope family can be seen here.

An Augustinian Priory was founded at Shelford in 1160, but suffered the fate proclaimed by Henry XII. Two thousand five hundred acres of land was then granted to Michael Stanhope. The Stanhopes lived in the manor house until the Parliamentarians set it alight during a surprise onslaught, and in the conflict, Colonel Stanhope was killed.

In more peaceful times the manor house was partially rebuilt.

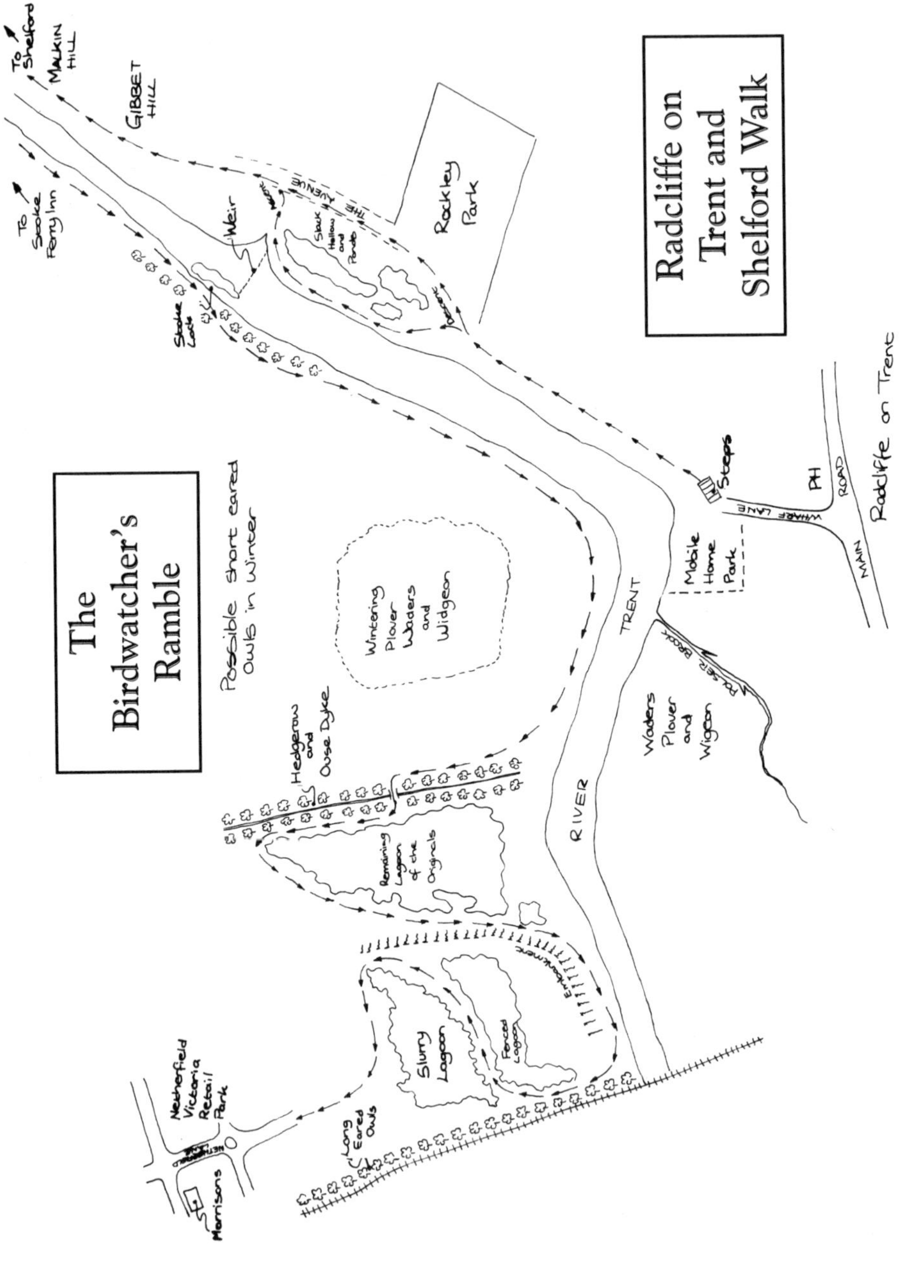
The Birdwatcher's Ramble
Radcliffe on Trent and Shelford Walk
To Shelford
MALKIN HILL
GIBBET HILL
To Stoke Ferry Inn
Weir
THE AVENUE
Stoke Hollow and Ponds
Rockley Park
Stoke Lock
Steps
PH
WHARF LANE
MAIN
ROAD
Radcliffe on Trent
Mobile Home Park
TRENT
RIVER
Polser Brook
Waders Plover and Wigeon
Wintering Plover Waders and Widgeon
Possible short eared Owls in Winter
Hedgerow and Ouse Dyke
Remaining Lagoon of the Originals
Embankment
Slurry Lagoon
Fenced Lagoon
Long Eared Owls
Netherfield Victoria Retail Park
Morrisons

The Birdwatcher's Ramble

Walk One: Stoke Bardolph to Netherfield

Walk Two: Stoke Bardolph to Gunthorpe

Map Reference:	OS Pathfinder 813 SK64/74 and 834 SK63/73
M1 Junction:	24 for Trent Bridge linking up with A612
Start:	Ferry Inn, Stoke Bardolph
Car Parking:	Ferry Inn area or the Estate Park, Stoke Lock
Buses:	Suggest you catch a Pathfinder 92 or 93 in Nottingham Old Market Square and alight at the Ferry Inn then walk to Netherfield and catch the Nottingham bound 92 or 93 at Morrisons supermarket, Victoria Park. There is no bus on Sunday.
Refreshments:	Ferry Inn, Stoke Bardolph. The Anchor Inn, Tom Browns, The Unicorn, The Toll House Restaurant, Gunthorpe
Distance:	2 miles direct route, $3\frac{1}{2}$ if exploring lagoons
Duration:	1-2 hours

About The Walk

Trainers may prove adequate in warm, dry weather but wear stout footwear at other times, if you intend to see something of the lagoons.

For the serious birdwatcher or wildlife enthusiast, recognition books, binoculars or 'scope' are essentials, although more gull and wader species are likely to be seen around the lagoon end of the walk.

In recent years, land reclamation has taken place here. The site was once recognised as an important feeding and breeding ground for wader species, and in 1945 made ornithological headlines when a pair of Black Winged Stilt successfully bred.

Red Footed Falcon and Great Reed Warbler have also been recorded here, and since the formation of the original Trent Valley Birdwatchers, the list of birds that have not been recorded here is probably considerably shorter than those that have!

The walk described follows the metalled road beside the River Trent to Stoke Lock, then continues before turning right and following a length of hedgerow before crossing the now fairly dry Ouse Brook for a progressive exploration of the Netherfield Lagoons. On the far side of these is the Victoria Retail Park, where you can board the S4 at Morrisons supermarket. Motorists, however, will need to retrace their steps to the car park.

The Route

The banks and bays of the Ferry Inn water attract twenty to thirty non-breeding mute swans, which come up the ramp and on to the grass to be fed. You can tell their age by the bill colourations. A swan up to two years sports a black bill, three years pink, four years red and five to adulthood, reddish orange. The bills of the old, past breeding birds, will be drab orange.

So to the road ahead. The metalled road takes you through a herd of Friesian Cattle to Stoke Lock and the Severn Trent/Stoke Bardolph car park.

The lock is now radio-operated and the lock-keeper's pleasant cottage tucked away to your right. Ash and sycamore provide a windbreak here, and the trees are regularly visited by all three species of woodpecker, nuthatch and treecreeper which fly across from the wooded cliffs at Radcliffe.

Herons often stilt along the path ahead or can be seen digesting their food or powdering and preening in the fields on either side of the waterway.

In the summer vetch and clovers pebbledash the ground and in the autumn and winter mixed flocks of plover — green, grey and the occasional golden — feed across the fields.

You will probably identify small birds such as meadow-pipits, redpolls, yellow-hammers, greenfinches, goldfinches, linnets and reed-buntings.

As we walk around the ninety-degree bend, pause to glass the Polser Brook field to the right of the mobile home park. In the winter, wigeon, plover, snipe and redshank can be seen, and oyster catchers also explore the runnels in the early spring.

Herons wade belly-deep in the shallows over there, and alongside, the resident swan pair use the shallows for anchoring and preening, and the field for grazing.

In the surface-edged willow branches of this nearside bank, both coot and great crested grebe pairs attempt to nest in the early year.

Eventually you will see the hedgerow on your right stretching, boundary fashion, almost to the track. As you close in, the broad track made by anglers' cars will appear. Leave the river and walk with the hedgerow to your left.

Expect the usual small birds along this route, but in the summer, visitors like the whitethroat and lesser whitethroat will be singing and holding breeding territories.

You never quite know what to expect here. Some years ago, I came across a large female tawny owl sunbathing, with her wings widely outspread around barley stalks, before she lifted swiftly from the crop and flew down the hedge. Blackbirds, mistle thrushes and great tits followed in mobbing pursuit.

Look for a plank bridge or hedge gap that will enable you to cross the Ouse Dyke, which in recent years, seems to have become a winterborne stream.

Having crossed, ahead of you are the Netherfield Lagoons. Follow one of the narrow winding paths to your right, with the water on your left, so that by rounding the lagoons you are also crossing the wide tract of rough field, making for the higher bank on the opposite side. This is where you need to have your binoculars and recognition book to hand.

One of the sightings that has lingered in my memory is that of a splendid greenshank cock which searched for food among the shallows. Reedstalks too one sultry July evening only twenty feet away. My late friend, Dick Barlow, a founder member of, and recorder for, the Trent Valley Birdwatchers, crossed this land tract almost daily when he was living and working in Netherfield, and were it not for him, I would never have become aware of just how rich and interesting a habitat this is.

Freshwater fish, amphibians, water and ground plant life, wildflowers, butterflies, daytime flying moths, small mammals and birds should hold your interest around these lagoons.

When you have reached the opposite side, and the embankment is on your right and the reedy backwaters on your left, ease along one of the narrow grass paths and return to the river path. Then turn right.

Check the high tension wires too, for twenty or thirty cormorants often preen up there after poaching trout from the nearby lakes in Colwick Country Park.

Just before you reach the railway bridge a short stiff climb can take you up the steep embankment to the barbed wire fence surrounding the next two tracts of water.

If you prefer, you can continue along the path and turn right just before the railway bridge, then walk with the railway embankment on your left to the entrance and access roads of Netherfield's Victoria Retail Park, and the Morrisons supermarket bus stop.

If you have decided to top the bank, then turn left, while keeping an eye on the water within the barbed wire enclosure. Years ago the lagoons here were on the same level as those you have walked round. But fortunately, the weed beds have remained and shine emerald green in the sunlight.

Both this stretch of water and the main fly ash pond, still out of sight, have been recently tenanted by an exceptionally fine pair of mute swans, the cob having been in the area since 1970.

The water before you now attracts gadwall, ruddy duck, tufted pochard, wigeon and goldeneye during the autumn and winter. Lapwings, snipe and redshank explore its margins, as do common and green sandpipers in the late summer.

You will see little and great crested grebe after they have dipped below the water surface, particularly on bright days. Notice how their underparts gleam silver between the weed beds, like the fish they seek.

During a spell of hard weather, you may see goosander also hunting. In summer, common terns will leave the course of the Trent to explore this shallow but beautiful stretch of water. Check the peninsulas, where in the early year redshank pairs perform their pre-copulation displays.

One early April morning, as I paused to check on the swan pair which were building the beginnings of their nest here, a squabbling group of canada geese slipped down a slope and collided with the startled cob, while just yards away rabbits were making off in all directions, a stoat in pursuit.

Over to your left is the railway embankment; the tall, thick stands of hawthorn attracting the titmice and finch species as well as the expected garden birds and raiders of the winter berry harvest, like the redwing and fieldfare.

A careful binocular or scope check is needed along this sheltered tract, for there is always the possibility of a long-eared owl or two using these thickets as a winter roost, regardless of the passing trains. All five British owl species are a possibility.

Where the paths divide, the bird enthusiast usually follows the embankment dividing the two fenced tracts of water, but if you are pressed for time you can continue ahead, then down the slope and round the white barrier to Morrisons. Over the traffic island and on the left, you will see the supermarket car park.

For those still on the walk, the fly ash water's edge to your left should yield a number of roosting and preening gulls and waders. No doubt a local birdwatcher or 'twitcher' will give you a list of the gull potential here. Usually it is the expected black-headed, common herring and greater and lesser black-backed which you see preening and regurgitating their pellets. When you have reached the end of the fly ash lagoon, keep it on your left.

When you have walked the inverted U of the fly ash embankment, you will see a gravel slope leading down to the path and white barrier, which is your exit point.

The short walk to Morrisons that I have just described is beyond this, but the car owner needs now to retrace his or her tracks to the river path and the car park.

Growing Popularity

In the 1960s only one man glassed these and the original lagoons in the lunch hour, and he was the late Dick Barlow.

One day he propped his old bicycle against a concrete post, birdwatched for an hour then returned on seeing bullocks gathered round. Reluctantly the bullocks withdrew as Dick approached. He found his bicycle on the

Peninsulas such as this are often worth "glassing" Photo T. Stevenson Collection.

ground trampled into an unrecognisable shape and with all the enamel licked from the frame!

Dick would have found himself in good company now, because birdwatchers employed at firms on the retail site come over in their lunch hour. Today between six and fourteen people can be seen here, but causing little disturbance to the wildlife and surrounding habitat.

Seasonal Walks

The Spring Walk

In the riverside willows and vegetation, look for the kingfisher pairs' interesting courtship displays. Early nests of great crested grebe will be attached to willows and alder roots between Stoke Lock and the railway bridge. The wake from passing boats washes to the sides of the anchored structures, and yet the eggs remain in the damp hollow.

You will find plover, redshank and the occasional greenshank, snipe and pied wagtails across the fields and in the dykes and runnels. Check for short and long eared owls. Barn owls are still a strong possibility.

The courtship displays of little grebe are almost as interesting as those of the great crested grebe. Chiff chaffs are usually the first migrants, with many willow warblers arriving about two weeks later. Stonechat, whinchat and wheatear are likely visitors, as are sedge-warbler, whitethroat and lesser whitethroat.

Garden warblers can occasionally be heard along the Radcliffe cliff walk, and you can expect to see and hear blackcaps and all three species of woodpecker. Swallows, house and sand-martins, yellow wagtails and little ringed plover will be looking for nest sites.

Redpolls visit Slack Hollow along with snipe and redshank. The main flowers by the Netherfield lagoon banks will be ladysmock and coltsfoot; later the various speedwells and bird's foot trefoil.

The Summer Walk

In June, all the previously mentioned warblers will be prevalent and sparrowhawk and kestrel will be competing for prey along with stoat, weasel and fox. You may also notice the sedge warbler cocks.

Freshwater fish species apparently found their way into the lagoons when the Trent was in flood. There have been some heavy and prolonged floodings throughout this section of the Trent Valley.

Most of the anglers regard the lagoons as being difficult to fish due to there being a wealth of natural food both below and on the water surface, but you may glimpse roach, rudd and occasional carp if you stand quietly around a bay or peninsula.

The daytime flying moths are legion here, especially the splendid burnets and lacewings. Butterflies are usually to be found close to their caterpillar food plants which, in the case of the peacock and small tortoiseshell, will be the stinging nettle beds, while the common blue favours the bird's foot trefoil. Patrolling butterflies like the orangetip and brimestone are occasionally to be seen, along with the various dragonflies of late summer.

By July, green and common sandpipers will be exploring the margins of the river and lagoons and you could glimpse the occasional pair of reed-warblers in the backwater pools below the fly ash embankment. Damsel flies are there too.

Just prior to its migrational flight, a young or adult cuckoo can sometimes be seen perched and preening on various fence posts on both sides of the river.

The Autumn Walk

Bird flocks will become noticeable now — starlings, meadow-pipits, goldfinches and fewer skylarks. 'Wisps' of snipe stay close to the marshy tracts.

Cygnets are flying at daybreak and circumventing their natal territories until around mid-October when they become adventurous, and either leave the area completely or join the non-breeding groups at Stoke and Trent Bridge before moving on. One or two of the females may stay around their natal territories, and attempt to breed there in later years.

Feral grey lag geese feed with the canadas and, when the berry harvests are at their peak, fieldfare, redwing and the occasional group of waxwing fly in and feed voraciously.

The early dusk could provide a memorable sighting of a barn owl, while little owl can be glimpsed at any time of day. On clear frosty nights male tawny owls, advertising their territorial boundaries, flute from the Radcliffe woods and the Stoke Lock sycamores. The flight patterns of finch and titmice flocks are worth studying. In the early autumn, merlin and hobby have been recorded, and later, common buzzard and peregrine.

The Winter Walk

Depending on weather and wind conditions, the bird list can become quite exhaustive. You may see scaup among all the expected wintering duck species, along with shelduck and oyster catchers.

At Netherfield, glass the hedgerow below and alongside the railway embankment for long-eared owl. Short-eared owls are not quite as frequent as they were twenty years ago, possibly due to the fluctuations in the small rodent populations.

Godwit enhance the wader species and whichever side of the river you are walking, the Polser Brook field just down from the Wharf Lane, Radcliffe-on-Trent mobile home site should not be ignored when glassing the runnels and marshy tracts. On clear starlit nights, you can hear the gabble talk of pink feet, as skeins of geese wheel down from the north and link the Trent's aquatic highway with their ancestral feeding grounds on the Isle of Axeholme and the Wash.

Walk Two
Ferry Inn to Gunthorpe

For a longer walk, take the downstream path around the Trent Ox-bow to Burton Meadows, and the riverside village of Gunthorpe beyond. In summer, the river's sandy margins attract a few waders, and of course, the occasional mute swan pair.

Anglers venture out in waders because, while there may not be as many chubb as they had hoped, there is always a chance of securing one of the 'fighting fish' or barbel.

The fields to the left of the ox-bow are know as Burton Meadows, and should be glassed by the birdwatcher, or moth enthusiast.

Carry on until you reach a footpath sign pointing across the fields. Turn here, with hedge to your right and farmland to your left. Notice the weavering hedge boundary. Eventually, you will see water gleaming between the willow branches on your right, for you are walking beside the most extensive of the Bulcote Ponds.

Various gulls, common tern, tufted duck, pochard and great crested grebe are usually to be seen here. Where the field boundaries merge, turn right with the hedgerow of blackthorn, hawthorn and elder thickets.

Continue walking to the next sign, which indicates that you are on a Severn Trent permissive path.

To your left, a wide track once used by gravel extraction lorries will take you directly to an anglers' car park, through a farm and cattle-grazed fields to Bulcote village and the main Nottingham-Burton Joyce-Lowdham road, which is open to you if you wish to take it.

To continue along the environmental route, however, take the track with the sheet of water still to your right and the embankment to your left. If you feel inclined to climb the embankment, you will see stretched below you another of the Bulcote Ponds, with banks acting as windbreaks, reedy peninsulas and three islands.

For about eight months of the year, from February until October, this stretch of water is usually tenanted by a mature pair of mute swans. The cob is undoubtedly the largest and heaviest swan for some miles. Between October and December, this pair join the bread-foraging flock at Stoke, then fly downriver to Trent Bridge until the breeding season comes round.

Continuing with your walk, all you need to do is keep the stretch of water to your right, and follow the wide track.

On the left is the tract of wild, broken land that divides the Bulcote Ponds from Gunthorpe Gravels. This is where I almost walked into my first short-eared owl when it rose from the grasses like a gigantic, round-eyed moth.

This first for me occurred in early April, so if you happen to be an owl enthusiast, then you could check such places as this throughout the autumn and winter months.

The track veers slightly left and away from the water, but bear with it so that the River Trent is again on your right. Go through or round the white gate, and continue down the narrow riverside track to Gunthorpe Bridge. You will see countless great crested grebe.

Spanning the Trent is Gunthorpe Bridge, which was opened by the Prince of Wales in 1927.

Willow, alder and haw thickets flank the next section of path for a few yards, then before you are the village green and moorings, now apparently combined. The Unicorn car park is ahead, Gunthorpe Lock and Weir alongside the Toll House Restaurant.

Now for some refreshments! The Anchor Inn, Tom Brown's Restaurant and the Unicorn Hotel are all within a stride of each other.

From here, it is back the way you have come. You need not, of course, skirt Bulcote Ponds, but continue back to Stoke with the river on your left.

Owl Associated Walks

In this Nottinghamshire section of the Trent Valley, I doubt that the Colwick to Gunthorpe area can be bettered, for tawny and little owls are widespread residents. Long-eared and short-eared owls are winter visitors, though they do take some finding.

I have an acquaintance who, on a later December afternoon, saw a little, short-eared and barn owl all within the space of ten minutes at Gunthorpe Bridge!

The occasional barn owl can be seen at Shelford and down the flood and gravel extraction areas to Gamston and Bassingfield. Both sides of the Lings Bar Road also provide adequate barn owl hunting grounds as do the fields in the vicinity of Silverdale, on the edge of Ruddington.

Ruddington also hosted between five and nine short eared owls during a particularly severe 'Russian snap' that occurred in the winter of 1986-87. The site at that time was maintained by the Royal Ordnance Factory, but today this area has become a recreational asset known as the Rushcliffe Country Park. The habitat is such that should a future rodent population explosion occur, these magnificent birds may return. And for you, the walker, it is just a matter of being there at the right time.

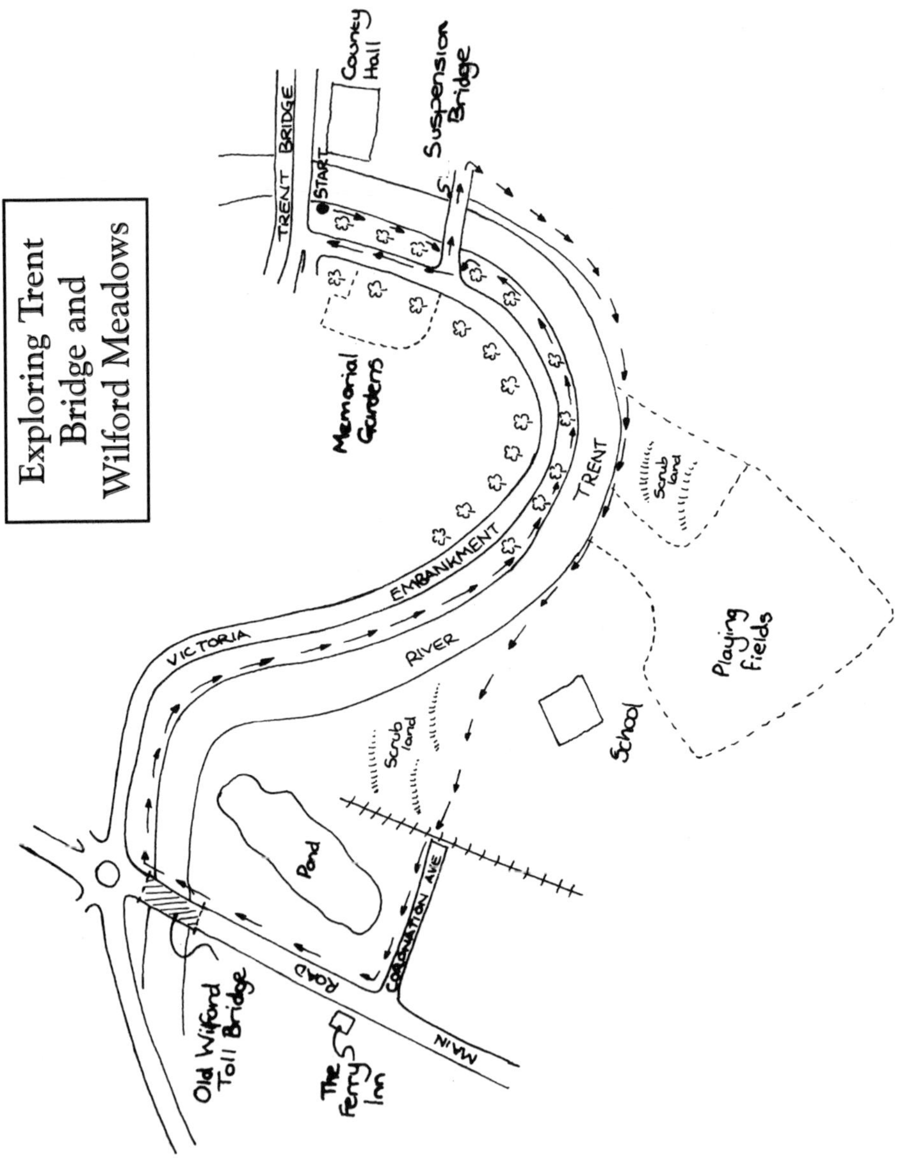
Exploring Trent Bridge and Wilford Meadows
County Hall
Suspension Bridge
TRENT BRIDGE
START
Memorial Gardens
Scrub land
VICTORIA EMBANKMENT
RIVER TRENT
Playing fields
School
Scrub land
Pond
CORONATION AVE
MAIN ROAD
Old Wilford Toll Bridge
The Ferry Inn

Trent Bridge and Wilford Meadows

M1 Junction:	24 for Trent Bridge
Distance:	2.5 miles
Duration:	1 hour
Start:	Trent Bridge — Victoria Embankment to Suspension Bridge
Car Parking:	According to roadside notice, but there is usually adequate space by the Victoria Embankment, Memorial Gardens
Buses:	From the various stops around Nottingham Market Square — 6, 9, 9A, 10, 12, 85
Refreshments:	The Ferry Inn, The Toll Bridge Inn

About The Walk

This route is an exploration of the riverside between Trent Bridge and the old Wilford Toll Bridge. It can be completed within an hour but the wildlife enthusiast will take longer to observe bird and mammal species.

The Route

If you decide to start at Trent Bridge rather than the Memorial Gardens, pause to look at the flood levels engraved in the north bank wall below The Aviary pub and path.

The arched structure of the present Trent Bridge has led historians to explore the possibility of there having been a bridge here about a thousand years ago.

There was certainly a bridge around 920-22, and a rebuilt bridge in 1156. In all probability these wooden structures were devastated by winter surges of floodwater.

1231 is the next date recorded in the construction of a Trent Bridge, and a few years later Royal consent was given for stone to be added. A decade later the superstructure was strengthened by working in timber, hewn from four Sherwood Forest oaks.

The bridge that we see today was originally forty feet wide and seventy feet long. There are four arches, but two further arches from medieval times can be seen in the sunken traffic island garden at the confluence of roads between the Trent Bridge Inn and County Hall.

The present bridge also serves as a memorial to Marriott Ogle Tarbotton, who designed it while employed as the city's first surveyor.

The current bridge was opened in 1871 and modified in 1925. The name Trent Bridge is also synonymous with the nearby Nottinghamshire County Cricket Club ground.

The Suspension Bridge is the next bridge down but as you are walking, notice the sweep of the fine embankment with its flanking lawns and avenue of lime and some London plane trees.

Notes on the wildlife species likely to be seen in accordance with the seasons can be found on the following pages.

Cross the Suspension Bridge, then turn right and walk the narrow path that takes you by the backs of the houses and the Rivermead flats.

Where the scrubland and derelict allotments begin is as good a place as any to see the city boundary rabbits. Here you can either take the top embankment, the riverside path or the paths snaking between the thickets towards the disused railway embankment.

Even as late as 1957-58 this tract of what is now scrubland was under water, and I well recall my Friday afternoons as an RAF conscript returning from Berkshire on the Bournemouth to Newcastle train, and seeing the white blaze of a swan on its nest in the reedbeds, its mate patrolling arch winged across the shining expanse. Yet today the entire area is walkable! The iron railway bridge under which you pass at Coronation Avenue serves as another memorial — to the Great Central Railway and the 1899 opening of Nottingham station.

The angling water to your right is known locally as Ironmongers Pond. Little grebe, heron and teal are sometimes disturbed here at first light.

At the tree junction, turn right, unless you decide to call at the Ferry Inn opposite. Progress along Main Road with more scrubland to your right, and cross the Wilford Toll Bridge.

There are still a few elderly folk who, on Saturday mornings, used to come here to watch the herds of cattle and sheep being driven over to the abattoirs around Great Freeman Street, London Road and Daleside Road.

Sign displayed outside the Toll Bridge House, Wilford

The livestock were driven by drovers who hired themselves and their bicycles out to the farmers each Saturday to take the cows and sheep to market.

Having crossed Wilford Toll Bridge, pause to study the sign above the shop which was once the tollkeeper's house.

Wilford Toll Bridge is an iron construction erected in 1870. Prior to this date there was a ferry at the site which seems always to have been a crossing place, judging by the number of interesting artefacts unearthed here, including, during the bridge's construction, Roman coins.

Turn right now and proceed along the fine Victoria Embankment to the Memorial Gardens, beyond the extensive sports fields on your left.

If you are a fountain and goldfish pool enthusiast, these gardens with their well-tended flower beds, gravel and paved terraces and rich variety of ornamental trees and shrubs should delay you for a few minutes, especially in May and June. The ornate entrance gates were erected and the gardens laid out to remind us of those who lost their lives in the First World War.

The statue of Queen Victoria was originally erected between The Bell Inn and the Odeon cinema in the centre of Nottingham, but was removed to its present site when the town planners decided to close Angel Row to through traffic.

The Spring Walk

Notice the behaviour patterns of the twenty to forty mute swans which congregate at various points along the Victoria Embankment steps. Those with brown patches on their plumage are cygnets, hatched the previous summer. The black-billed birds will be a year older and the pink-billed in their third year.

Regardless of whether the 'berry' at the base of the bill has formed or not, the sex ratio in any swan flock is about three males to one female, and the same can be said for most species of waterfowl.

These swans are non- or pre-breeders, but you will see the youngsters forming pairing bonds.

Sexes can be told apart because the male or 'cob' sits higher on the water surface than the female or 'pen'. Watch them facing one another and indulging in tapering-necked courtship routines.

Occasionally, two youngsters pairing in this manner will be driven away by a dominant cob, who will pursue them with wings arched over his back. In all probability, this bird will have a mate feeding nearby and be demonstrating his aggression. Eventually, this mature pair will select a choice breeding territory; usually away from the river.

The Canada geese are also pairing, and again you will see dominant ganders flying at and attempting to break up, the newly formed pairs. By doing this the dominant ganders are instinctively attempting to reduce the competition for choice breeding territories.

The many feral mallard are fairly recent riverside itinerants, some of which will probably be on the Nottingham Arboretum pond one day, and at University Park the next.

A pair or two occasionally nest in a window box, high above the streets of the Lace Market, and pairs prospecting for a nest site can also be seen on the fountain ponds in front of the Council House and the small fish pond in the Castle grounds.

Notice the head-nodding motions of the mallard duck as she courts the drake of her choice. On the steps you may also see the occasional pair of chaffinches and pied wagtails.

After crossing the Suspension Bridge and turning right, you will notice the expected garden birds, then just by the Rivermead flats the coot pairs will be establishing their territories throughout the stretches of river bank reed beds, elder and willow thickets.

It is worth pausing here to watch the rabbits foraging in the bramble thickets and in the allotments to your left. As with the birds, there is a definable pecking order.

The scrubland thickets between here and Coronation Avenue should yield sightings of linnet, yellow-hammer, bullfinch, dunnock, blue, great and long-tailed tits and fewer willow or marsh-tits.

Migrants like the chiffchaff, willow-warbler, grasshopper-warbler, whitethroat, lesser whitethroat, whinchat, swallow, house and sand-martin, swift and cuckoo can also be added to the list and, in April, wheatears returning to breed in the Derbyshire hill country.

The riverside should continue to provide sightings of reed-bunting, coot, moorhen, little grebe, great crested grebe, kingfisher and heron. Cormorants also follow the riverway making to or from the Attenborough Reserve to pillage stock from the troutlake at Colwick Country Park.

In recent years, cormorants have also fished the stretch between Trent Bridge and the Suspension Bridge, but always with the swans and canada geese providing a barrier between themselves and the people walking or angling along the Embankment.

The Summer Walk

Early morning visitors to the scrubland area may well glimpse a vixen seeking food for her cubs. I have a vivid recollection of travelling on the upper deck of a Wilford Lane bus around midday, and seeing a splendid dog-fox loping through the grasses and stopping occasionally to roll like a dog or cat.

There will be rabbits of all sizes here and occasionally one of the stoats, the predator of rabbits, may be glimpsed hunting and stalking.

The scrubland thickets will still provide habitat for the previously mentioned bird species, although those passing through like the swift and cuckoo, will have left by early August.

Turning and twisting in flight as they prospect for small fish while following the course of the river, are the common terns. Notice how each one spiral dives in its efforts to seize its prey.

If you have a butterfly or moth recognition book with you, why not sit on the Embankment steps for a while and attempt to identify some of the daytime flying moths hovering over the submerged steps?

One that you will easily recognise is the peppered moth, which, as the late Dr. Bernard Kent pointed out, survives better because the dark form of a moth in an industrial environment is less easily located and picked off by birds, although when seen against the water it is very noticeable.

Along the submerged steps there are large shoals of minnow and stickleback. Watch them foraging in and over the algae beds.

The mute swans, like the canada geese and mallard, are moulting and flightless, the year old cygnets and 'pen' swans in June/July and the cobs July/August. Yet still a strict pecking order is maintained throughout each interchanging group.

By listening to these fine birds, you will soon conclude that the name 'mute' is a misnomer and a pair in particular will give out a series of rasping 'aun-aun' notes or the occasional 'isp' and sharp warning grunt.

If a dominant cob displays and sees off the swans around him, when he returns to his mate he will sidle alongside, with wings raised and bill-tip to the sky and give out a series of deep trumpet notes which end in a sonorous purr. This behaviour sequence continues throughout the year.

The Autumn Walk

Although the summer migrants have left, the night sky above the city and river serves as a flyway for migrating waders, rails, herons, duck like the wigeon, pochard and scaup, geese and swans. Unfortunately the Victoria Embankment lawns and those in front of County Hall attract the canada geese flocks in to graze and preen. Some of these geese have bred or been reared locally, while others may have known the Derbyshire and Staffordshire parks, the Cheshire meres and Humber estuary.

The mute swan breeding pairs from the Colwick, Holme Pierrepont and Ruddington country parks will introduce their cygnets to the Trent as a means of dispersing them. Rival breeding pairs arch their wings in the aggressive display known as 'busking' and temporary territories are sometimes established. When the cold weather comes in, the aquatic vegetation is of little benefit to them, so the swans will accept your handouts of brown bread, lettuce and grain which you scatter along the steps for other birds.

In the scrub area, notice how the linnets and yellow-hammers are flocking. You may well see a sparrowhawk harrying these and the starling flocks, and sometimes a kestrel or little owl intent on a similar mission.

You will probably disturb pairs and trios of pied wagtails from the embankment steps and thickets. The nearby playing fields will also host flocks of fieldfare and redwing, those intriguing thrushes from the north.

When perched high, fieldfares are distinctive as they all face the same direction — into the wind.

Two or three grey wagtails are often to be seen along the Victoria Embankment, and the waterside thickets near Wilford Toll Bridge provide anchorage for the occasional water-rail.

The Winter Walk

Notice how the dominant mute swan cobs are displaying and exercising aggression as they compete for food, as are the canada ganders.

Gulls, namely the black headed, common and sometimes a herring gull or lesser-black backed, will be foraging along the river, and now is as good a time as any to compare them in the bird recognition book.

During the snow follow the trails of the rabbits and the foxes, which cover quite a distance.

There are still grebe and cormorants on the river and there is a good chance of seeing a kingfisher. Sparrowhawk, kestrel and an occasional merlin will follow the small bird flocks over Wilford Meadows and the scrub area, and at nightfall a barn owl sometimes puts in an appearance.

Walk One
Bulwell Hall Park

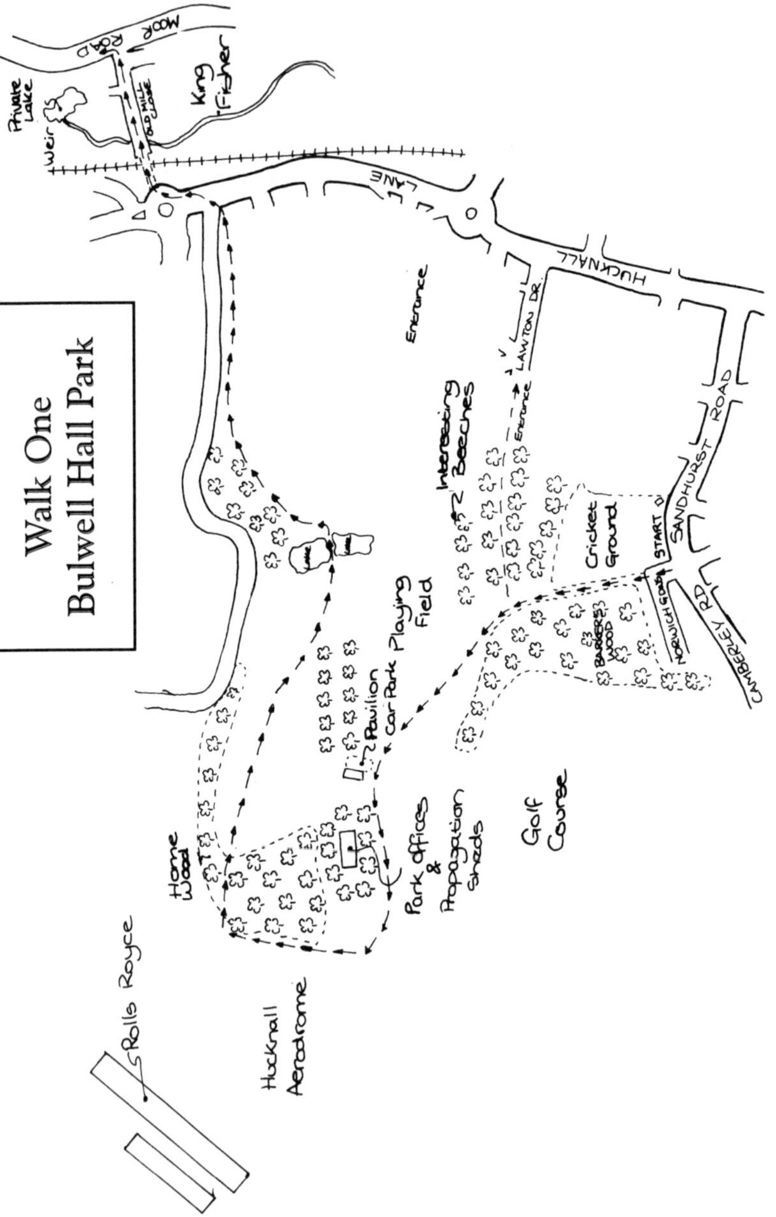

Three Walks Around Nottingham's Urban Fringe

Walk One
Bulwell Hall Park

M1 Junction:	26 for A6002
Map Reference:	OS Pathfinder 812 SK 44/54
Start:	Park's main entrance, Norwich Gardens, Bulwell
Car Parking:	Two car parks. One near the sports pitches on the right. The other way down by the changing rooms. On an evening visit you need to check the park closing time displayed on the board by the gate.
Buses:	**Walk One** — From Queen Street, Central Nottingham — 72/72B. On Sundays enquire at Bulwell Bus Station **Walk Two** — Beginning at Forge Mills— Hucknall Bypass — from Beastmarket Hill — 79, but not on Sunday
Refreshments:	Suggest you pack your own for these three walks or on Walk Three call at the Bestwood Lodge Hotel.
Duration:	1-2 hours walk or day or half day
Distance:	**First walk**. Approx 1¾ miles **Second walk** Approx 1¾ miles **Third walk** Approx 2-2½ miles. **Total** Approx 5-5½ miles

About The Walks

These routes can either be walked separately or combined as a day or half day exploration of the entire urban fringe area, whether you intend to seek out wildlife and aspects of local history, or just walk for the love of it. You will cover a few miles, because the walks are fairly circular and connected.

The Route

Squires Avenue, connecting the centre of Bulwell to the park entrance, probably resembled Lime Tree Avenue in Wollaton Park at the beginning of the century, although it is difficult to imagine this today. Once you are inside the park boundary, Barkers Wood to your left is often worth an exploration, if only to glimpse the grey squirrels. Unfortunately, sycamores have been allowed to self-regenerate here but there are still some pleasant stands of silver birch, broom and bramble thicket. Ground ivy and dog's mercury provide most of the ground cover, along with carpets of oak leaves. There are still a few fine oaks, beech, horse and sweet chestnut trees to provide varied food and habitats for the birds and small mammals. Woodcock are not unknown, for the area has damp thicketed hollows in which these large inland waders love to probe beneath the ground surface for worms and insects. Several ponds and fields are out of sight, but close to Blenheim Lane on the other side of the golf course, so the entire area will attract woodcock, especially in the autumn and winter.

The paths wind through the wood to the edge of the golf course, which should be on your left if you are making your way back to the main drive.

Other local feathered residents are the tawny owls. When we lived locally, I used to bring my son here just to listen to them fluting at dusk. On frosty winter nights I have stepped from the porch of the Hall Park Tavern, almost opposite the park entrance, and heard tawnies fluting in unison as each male advertised his territorial boundary.

The pellets of these nocturnal hunters can often be sorted from the leaf litters at the foot of the mature trees throughout the park, for these owls change their roosts regularly, and in the colder months will use the cypresses, yews and tall evergreen shrubs in which to roost by daylight.

Having returned to the main drive, turn left. The five beeches to your right make an interesting study, especially the variations in bark patterns.

Swing left again, with the golf course to your left and, facing oncoming traffic, walk to the changing rooms, propagation sheds, outbuildings and courtyards of the manor house site. The house was knocked down some years ago. Today, attempts would have been made to restore it, for it was a fine and well-planned country seat. The trees in the grounds here are impressive. There are toilets adjacent to the new changing rooms, and a childrens' playground at the end of the car park.

If you are exploring the path beside the hall grounds, there are various conifers including Scots pine and cypresses. In fact, the evergreens are as numerous as the deciduous trees. Note the holly hedge to your right, and a leaf-filled ditch below a low wall, which in years gone by could have served as a ha-ha or short section of ornamental moat.

The buildings are surrounded by a splendid stand of pine, and although the public are not admitted beyond that point, you can stand and look straight down the drive to the formal entrance of the outbuildings.

This outer path bypasses still more extensive gardens with lawns to your right, then turns a corner by the golf course on your left.

Again there are some fine mature spinneys.

For the wildlife enthusiast most of the expected parkland and woodland birds are here, and also include wheatear and redstart passing through as migrants. Swallows and house martins are regular summer breeders. Pairs of spotted flycatcher breed here too. These little birds fit well into the niches provided by old walled country houses, gardens and courtyard walls in need of maintenance. So by standing quietly in this area in May, you will probably locate them. Consult your bird recognition book if you want more general information on the species.

Connected to this corner of the park is the footpath divided in parts by a hedgerow, and bordering Hucknall Airfield.

By turning left, you can follow this to Hucknall or progress across Blenheim Lane, Bulwell and take up with it again by Bulwell Wood; then continue to Nuthall.

On the airfield itself, the birdwatcher may see skylark, wheatear, yellow-hammer, meadow-pipit, yellow wagtail, snipe, lapwing and, in the

The ride leading down to the sportsfield and lakes at Bulwel Hall Park

winter, flocks of fieldfare and redwing. A retired employee of Rolls Royce once mentioned having watched a pair of mute swans attempting to land on the rain-soaked runways, which they obviously mistook for channels of deep water.

The impact of their landing caused the swans to roll over on their backs for some yards, before they sat stunned and disorientated for half an hour before taking off again. One sustained a leg injury that since has proved a considerable handicap.

If you follow the lane to the right you may find a hedgegap that will bring you back into the park and across the tract of interesting land known as Home Wood. If, however, the gap has been filled in, then you need to retrace your steps by the outbuildings and gardens to the toilet block and changing rooms.

For the direct walker a route stretches ahead from the car park, down the grove of trees and between two football pitches, to the lakes and the path dividing them.

For those with time to explore Home Wood, go by the back of the changing room block.

The Home Wood tract is still a wilderness where most of the British finch species, the usual titmice, including long tailed tit and bunting species like the yellow-hammer, corn and reed-bunting, may by glimpsed.

On summer mornings and evenings, all this area and the railway embankment resounds with the songs of willow-warblers, whitethroats and lesser whitethroats. Grasshopper-warbler and cuckoo add their contrasting voices to the choir. In April and May the ground is starred with the pretty, violet blue, trailing flowers of the periwinkle. Coltsfoot also abounds here. Poppies thrive alongside bluebells and whitebells, various members of the speedwell family, and, from April to June, clumps and beds of ramsons, or wild garlic, with flower heads gleaming like stars within the mass of broad leaves and grass stems.

From Home Wood we next need to cross to the middle path of the lakes. Notice how rich in weed the small stretches of water are. Besides the usual freshwater fish, it is these weed beds which attract the mute swans in to feed.

Before exploring the middle path, look in the water immediately to your right, close to the corner of the bank, for it is here that young pike can sometimes be seen, particularly in the early morning. There is usually a coot family in residence and in times when the lakes were not so well-used, I have known a pair of little grebe or dabchick attempt to nest here.

At the end of the middle path, turn left and follow the lakeside round by the reed bed. There is usually a mute swan pair nesting here. The pen of the current pair arrived as a blackbilled youngster, one of a brood of five cygnets hatched at nearby Mill Lake in 1995. The cob is an exceptionally large bird. The unfortunate thing about the reed bed is its proximity to the bank, for it also attracts louts with guns, and the cruelties inflicted upon the swan pair and their eight newly hatched cygnets in 1996 made headlines in both the local and national press. Swan pairs may leave, but others will come in, because these rich feeding grounds extend along a flight line connecting the lakes of north Nottinghamshire to the Trent and Erewash valleys.

The narrow inlet at the top end is a good place to look for a kingfisher. Some of my most memorable early morning sightings have occurred here. You need now to take the path threading between the willows, sycamores and alders to the field path.

Having done this, Hucknall Aerodrome should be on your left, the railway embankment on your right. From here, you need to turn to Walk Two.

If, however, you are content with that one exploration of Bulwell Hall Park, then it is just a matter of retracing your steps to the car park or bus stop.

A Brief History of Bulwell Hall

Built by Mr John Newton in 1770, Bulwell Hall was eventually enlarged by the Reverend Charles Padley and T.S. Cooper.

Surprisingly, more has been recorded about the grounds than the interior of the house, although we are informed that fine paintings 'by ancient and modern masters' were privately exhibited along the staircase and galleries. The two small lakes that we see today may once have been one lake of seven acres.

Special references were made to the parkland timbers and the ornamental planting which continued to take place. The lake and the park comprised 200 acres.

In 1890, the estate was bought by the Rector of Bulwell, Thomas Hardy. When he died it seems there was no successor, so the Home

Office opened the house as a sanatorium for children suffering from tuberculosis. Later it became Army Headquarters and remained so until 1947.

By 1957 the Hall was described as being in a very dilapidated state with windows boarded up, the kitchen gardens and drives overgrown and almost beyond recognition. Local legend tells us that the clock in the tower stopped at 7.00pm when Nottingham was targeted by German bombers during the war.

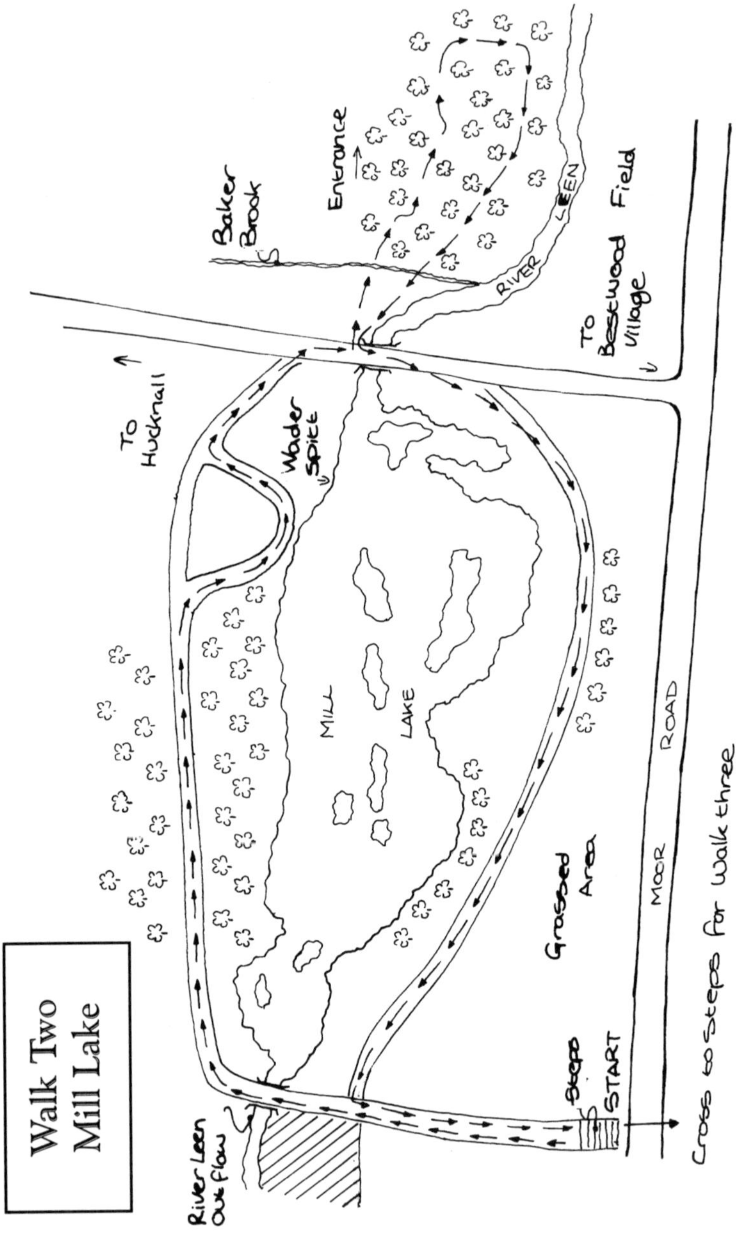
Walk Two
Mill Lake
River Leen Out flow
Steps
START
Cross to steps for Walk three
MOOR ROAD
Grassed Area
MILL LAKE
Wader Spike
To Hucknall
Baker Brook
Entrance
RIVER LEEN
Field
To Bestwood Village

Walk Two
Mill Lake

Start: Embankment steps entrance to the Mill Lake site Moor Road/B683

Buses: From Beastmarket Hill, Nottingham — 79. On Sunday from Nottingham Victoria Centre — 141

Car Parking: Continue along B683 to Park Road on the right

For The Motorist

Follow Park Road until you reach the official car park to Bestwood Country Park. Walk down Park Road, then turn left. Cross and continue along the pavement until you reach the embankment steps. Go up these. The walk begins beyond Bulwell Hall.

For The Walker

Leaving the Bulwall Hall lake by the feeder stream path at the top end, make your way through the willow and silver birch woodland, where there is a clearly defined path, which you need to follow to the gap in the disused railway embankment.

For the wildlife enthusiast it is worth scanning the fields for both green and wintering golden plover, all the expected finch species, meadow and tree pipits, and, during migration, redstarts, wheatears and whinchats.

The embankment provides a home for several fox cub litters and, of course, long tailed fieldmice and bank voles.

Follow the path beyond the embankment and down towards Bulwell. Sadly, the path has become unsightly, but was a very pleasant hedgeside track thirty or forty years ago.

Where the path joins the Main Road, notice the thread of a stream near the fence. Students catching a bus here to Hucknall have often watched an early morning heron hunting for frogs within yards of the streaming traffic. You need now to cross the main road and turn left. Walk by the bus shelter, the little pool and seat area to your right.

Take the narrow path leading up to the railway line and take care — this line is now in use and is the Newstead Abbey and Mansfield line. Once across the railway notice the privately-owned mill pool, the weir and the River Leen to your left, and the animal feed processing plant to your right with the roughland and willow thickets beyond.

This is barn owl country and one owl can occasionally be seen hunting here in the deep winter dusk.

Most of the river and railwayside between Newstead and the main Bulwell shopping centre comprises derelict fringe land and waterlogged thickets and is hunting ground for both barn and little owl.

Notice the structure and stonework positioning of the buildings called Forge Mills to your left. Though the date remains unclear, the mills are believed to have been built by the monks of Newstead.

To your right a channel cuts along by the buildings and the field edge. Scan the overhanging branches here for kingfishers. The field to your right is also private property, but using binoculars in the lane can sometimes prove worthwhile for the small bird enthusiast.

There is a private residence to your left, then farm buildings which are now used as storage sheds. One elderly resident can still recall the times when free range poultry, ducks and geese were sprawled across this lane and the cows herded down twice daily for milking. This lane now becomes Old Mill Close.

Turn left at the end, and walk the Moor Road pavement until you reach the steps in the embankment to your left. This is a haw thicket and scrubby area, So don't miss them. There is also a newly built bridge.

After climbing these steps you are at the beginning of...

Walk Two

Here the path needs to be followed to the Leen outflow from Mill Lake and beyond. Notice the two or three Highland Cattle in the field below and on your left and pause to take in the careful planning and conservation which have so admirably replaced the previous waste tip and Leen backwater.

There are several islands, all of which held only saplings when the site was being designed and worked in 1981/82. The entire stretch of water from end to end was windswept. Now the trees serve as windbreaks and wildlife habitats and remain, in my opinion, unrivalled throughout the county.

River Leen Backwater Mill Close, Bestwood

Once you have turned the bend, notice all the tree species in the plantations to your left and right, the majority bearing autumn and winter berry harvests to feed the visiting fieldfares, redwings, mistle, song thrushes and blackbirds.

The tall house on the opposite side of the water is a private residence, but it was once a mill house. The River Leen may have originally cut its way much closer to the house and road than the lake bank of present times suggests.

While you are here, take in the undulating green fields over to your left contrasting with the row of rooftops marking the cul-de-sac known as The Spinney. The gentle ridge progresses in this manner to Goosedale. When you continue to the fence gate at the lane, go through the opposite fence gate to continue your walk in the Bestwood Country Park area.

The thread of water here is known as the Baker Brook, and joins the Leen just beyond the bridge and over to your right.

This is really a loop track walk that finishes at the tubular gate and hedgerow bordering private land, over which horses and ponies are occasionally grazed.

The Leen however nurtures some lovely sandy bays along here. The farmyard ducks find these attractive and, in the season, marsh marigolds or 'kingcups' bring dashes of colour to the waterside banks. Again, this is private land.

You are now in a cul-de-sac but there are several paths from which to choose. Notice the splendid plantations. The River Leen is over to your left, often just out of sight, but the quiet walker can sometimes be rewarded with the glimpse of a kingfisher.

Returning to the fence gate, go through it, turn left, and over the Leen. Then go through the fence gate and back to the lakeside, with the Leen inflow to your right.

Whether or not you are a wildlife enthusiast, you will hardly fail to notice the swans, canada geese and small waterfowl gathered here. The grassy peninsula across from the millhouse is the place where most of the local folk stand and throw their offerings to the swans and geese.

If you follow the path with the lake to your right, notice the willow thicket and pool area to your left. Where the path gently turns, the locked gate and fence and thicket area are again to your right. This is surely very old waterlogged ground following the original bed of the River Leen, the narrow banks of which can be seen over the fence, as the slope that you walked earlier comes into sight.

At the Leen outflow, turn left, up the slope and down the steps, then carefully cross the busy Moor Road to the opposite steps and the beginning of Walk Three.

Seasonal Highlights of the Mill Lake Site

Spring Walk

Scan the alder, reed and phragmites area below the fence to your left. All the titmice species, including marsh and the very occasional willow tit, may be seen along the tree line. Reed-buntings will be indulging in their courtship chases and by May, the adults will be carrying food for their young. Water-rail are not unknown here and moorhens and mallard are common. Canada pairs will sometimes nest and bring their goslings up to Mill Lake.

The private field can yield early morning glimpses of snipe, woodcock, lapwing and yellow wagtail. Look for yellow-hammers on the fence posts. Perhaps in April there will be a wheatear or whinchat.

The thickets may seem hampered by early foliage but many of the small bird species will be food-seeking here. The occasional cuckoo will also patrol this area and the railway embankment thickets over to the left. Chiff-chaff, willow-warbler and blackcap share the same habitat.

Swallows, house-martins and occasional sand-martins hunt for flying insects, and the small emerald bird skimming between the islands or over the Leen bridge could well be a kingfisher.

Great crested and little grebe, coot, moorhen and ruddy duck breed here as do the vastly over-populating pairs of canada geese. In recent years, two pairs of mute swans have successfully reared cygnets. Previously, a young cob and pen who hatched off a brood of seven on the Forge Mill private lake daily escorted their brood up the path and on to Mill Lake where territorial disputes took place with the resident pair.

You will see kestrels hovering, and may glimpse a sparrowhawk around the islands. Perhaps there is a 'plucking block' here.

Tufted duck have bred, but only occasionally, and still seem to be regular visitors. Herons use the trees for preening, and roosts, from which they regurgitate their pellets.

Winter light: the River Leen flowing into Mill Lake, Bestwood

Summer Walk

All the breeding duck, moorhens, coot and grebe pairs will be out with their broods, and when not feeding and preening, the rival mute swan cobs will be patrolling their territorial lines.

July and August is the time of the moult. Many drakes of the dabbling duck species will be dingy-looking now but can still be identified by their bill and body shape. The breeding mute swan pens will moult in June/July and be full-winged six weeks later. The cobs will then begin their moult.

Keep scanning elsewhere for small birds and raptors.

Autumn Walk

Scan the phragmites area and private field again for snipe, woodcock and possible water rail. By October the first fieldfares and redwings will be feeding through the berry thickets. On mild days, robins break into territorial song. The robin is unique in that the females also sing. Most of the summer visitors will be gone, although you may glimpse over-wintering warblers like chiffchaff and blackcap.

Cygnets will be flying at first light, often returning with the pen, after a circuitous route has been formed. Late-reared cygnets will be browner than those hatched earlier, which have more white in their plumage.

Non-breeding swans, usually two and three year olds, will also fly in and be chased by the dominant pairs. Canada geese will also be flying between different stretches of water. You may see common sandpiper and redshank around the gravelly margins of the islands. Teal and scaup duck are not unknown. The occasional merlin may, like the sparrowhawk, seek the seclusion of the island trees.

Winter Walk

When you have climbed the steps, scan the tree line to your left, particularly the alders, for here siskin can often be seen feeding on the cones. Grey wagtails will frequent the lakeside. Notice how the number of ducks on the lake has built up, according to weather conditions.

A few wigeon pass through and in the hawthorn thickets a long-eared owl may roost by daylight. In really hard weather, the fieldfare and redwing flocks will bring that 'Northern reminder' to the thickets as they fly in to feed on the berry harvests. Continue to note the behaviour patterns of common waterfowl like the canada geese and mute swans.

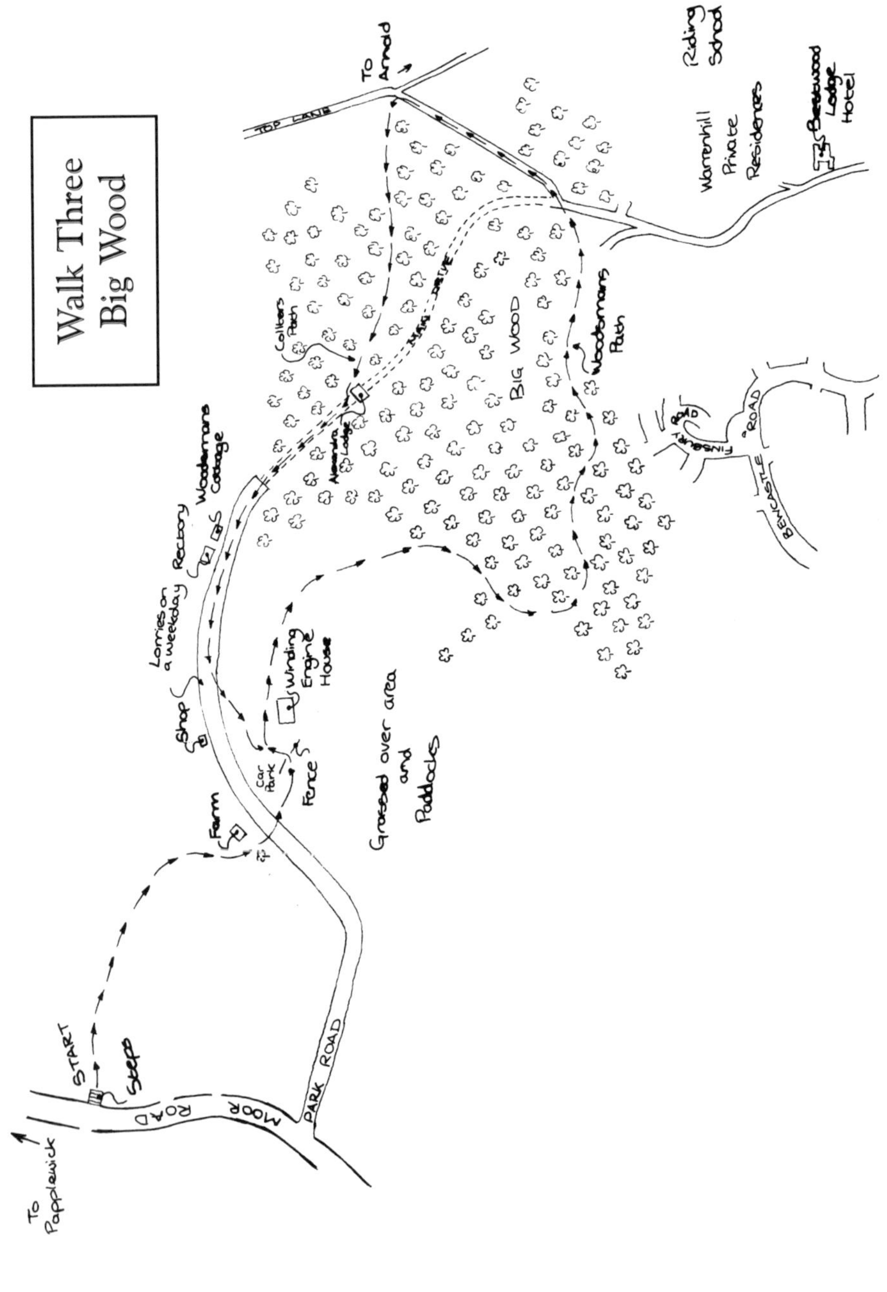
Walk Three
Big Wood
To Arnold
TOP LANE
Riding School
Warrenhill Private Residences
Bestwood Lodge Hotel
Colliers Path
MAIN DRIVE
BIG WOOD
Alexandra Lodge
FINSBURY ROAD
BEWCASTLE ROAD
Rectory
Lorries on a weekday
Shop
Winding Engine House
Car Park
Fence
Farm
Grassed over area and Paddocks
START
Steps
MOOR ROAD
PARK ROAD
To Papplewick

Walk Three
Big Wood

Leave the lake site by the steps at the Leen outflow end, and at the bottom of the steps, cross Moor Road. This is a fast road.

Proceed up the steps opposite and follow the track threading along the top of the embankment. The old British Coal Board offices and storage compounds are to your left, Moor Road with its traffic below to your right, but only for a short distance.

Bestwood residents returning late along this winding road on a winter night mention having occasionally seen a barn owl hunting here.

The trees are mainly self-regenerated sycamore and hawthorn, with bulky magpie nests in these thickets. The small birds are likely to be meadow-pipits, skylarks, bullfinch, greenfinch, goldfinch and linnets.

Eventually, silver birches become more prominent than the sycamores, and gorse and broom begin to appear. Down on your left is the private residence, Forge Farm. It has a tunnel entrance beneath the tract of embankment over which you are walking. Walk on a little further past the farm, and you will reach another track segmented to your left.

Cross on to this so that Forge Farm is again on your left, and continue along the path to the gated boundary of the country park.

Ahead are two tracks. The slender one is the horse trail. The wider one is for you, the walker.

This broken tract of land is really valuable as wildlife habitat and as long as there are thriving populations of field or bank vole there will be birds that prey on them, such as sparrowhawk, kestrel, little and barn owls.

A few yards on, and you will become aware of grass and fenced paddock areas to the right. Now try to imagine a great mountain of grey colliery slurry here. That is exactly what would have met the eye many years ago. We have the foresight of the Nottinghamshire County Council Countryside Divisions planners and contractors to thank for the change that has taken place since the beginning of the 1980s, for all this is now part of Bestwood Country Park.

Ahead on the left, the colliery winding house is coming into view; a landscaped area; and a car park which again is a recent addition purchased from the Coal Board. In fact it is an area that could scarcely be envisaged when the Country Park was in its inaugural stages throughout 1982-86.

Take the path that swings sharply left towards this landscaped area and ease through the pedestrian gap in the barbed wire fence. To continue the walk, bear right towards the winding house. If you want to leave the route entirely, cross the landscaped area to the bus shelter on Park Road.

The bus from here to Bulwell, Nottingham and Clifton is the No. 70. The incoming bus turns just by here then picks up passengers bound for Hucknall. Please note however, that there is no bus on Sundays or Bank Holiday Mondays.

The winding house understandably interests the local industrial archaeology enthusiasts and notes relating to it can be found at the Alexandra Lodge Ranger headquarters. For many years the colliery cage, pit baths and National Coal Board storage depots dominated this immediate area.

In March, coltsfoot and celandine abound. A pair of kestrels and little owls were breeding close by and as neighbours throughout the 1980s.

Leaving the winding house, there are stands of broom and gorse close by. Over to the right the treeline along the bottom of the hill provides forage for finches, titmice, fieldvoles and long tailed fieldmice.

To the left of the sandtrack, there are small paddocks divided by post-and-rail fencing. Further along, various small but progressive oaks contrast with the white-trunked silver birches, gorse, broom and ground flora.

This is a morning place, and although you may meet the occasional walker or jogger, I never fail to enjoy the silence, except in the summer when all the songbirds are in chorus. Besides the usual robins, wrens, and accentors, the banks attract the expected finch and titmice species, yellow-hammer and the occasional pair of tree pipits or whinchat.

Gradually, the track changes, as bramble masses and stands of self-regenerated sycamore take over the slopes. Ahead, as the track divides, lodgepole pine and whitebeam saplings catch the eye and there are direction signs for the horse trail and Alexandra Lodge.

Notice the natural sandstone shelving to the left, holding the roots of gorse and broom. Continue following this track, threading between the silver birches, sycamores and brambles.

This has always been a popular breeding area of that colourful member of the crow family, the jay, and an occasional nest can be seen, usually wedged into a tree fork between twelve and forty feet from the ground. The jay's alarm call is a low but prolonged screech.

During the autumn, quite a number of these birds can be seen foraging for acorns and beechmast throughout the woods.

Stands of yew become more apparent as the track turns. Your route now is optional. You can take any one of the paths, but to continue with this walk you need to be heading uphill and out of the valleys.

The route I do not recommend is the one which looks the easiest — the narrow green track — for it ends in a very steep climb up to the high periphery path. My advice is to continue following the sandtrack winding up the slopes.

Despite the lack of mature timber, there are still a few oaks, and at the top of the slope path there is another stand of yew which makes a good roost for small birds and tawny owls in particular.

The slopes are swathed with bracken and more than one litter of fox-cubs has been reared to maturity here in comparatively recent times. Around the sycamores and silver birches, the autumn photographer and fungi hunter will no doubt be delighted with the colourful, but poisonous, fly agaric that flares from the carpets of grass, leaves and mosses.

Having reached the top of the slope, turn left, on to the Woodman's Path and continue walking with the little valleys of sycamore, yew, oak and chestnut opening up below. Rowan or mountain ash, hazel and holly saplings can also be seen.

All three species of woodpecker and nuthatch thrive in these woodland pockets, which is one reason I have chosen this route.

The drummings of both the lesser and greater spotted woodpeckers accompany the walker on spring and early summer mornings and the 'laughing' call of the green woodpecker or 'yaffle' echoes through the glades.

There are still a few mature oaks along this ridge. Notice the five or six nest boxes which, in season, each hold a breeding tenant. Tree sparrow, nuthatch and greater spotted woodpecker use these. If you are fortunate in locating a woodpecker hole that has been made by a breeding pair, do not expect the pair to use the same hole the following year. It will not, however, remain untenanted, for in all probability a starling pair will take it over.

The paths divide, but the Woodman's Path is the one to the right which follows the park boundary, bypassing the school playing fields to your right.

A small watercourse threads down for a few yards. Local children will tell you that frogs are common in March and April. Small birds, of course, drink here.

There are many sycamore stands. Continue along this track to the corner fence and country park entrance, then turn left with the private grounds to your right. For refreshment, you need to turn right and walk a few hundred yards to the Bestwood Lodge Hotel, then rejoin the route here.

Alternative Route

When you reach the Main Drive you can either continue down to Alexandra Lodge, or turn right along the drive for another interesting detour.

The Alexandra Lodge Route

Continue down the winding track. When the Nottinghamshire County Council rangers first moved in, this was a stoney and uneven route, closely fringed by bracken, gorse and bramble. Bird enthusiasts will recognise all the usual species here, especially summer-visiting warblers like the chiffchaff, willow-warbler and blackcap. Tree creeper may be glimpsed and magpie nests are as common as the grey squirrel dreys.

This track was the estate's main drive which led from the Bestwood Park entrance known as Alexandra Lodge to the country house on the hilltop, surrounded by trees and now called the Bestwood Lodge Hotel.

The drive ahead is now fenced either side. It was a derelict track leading down by Woodman's Cottage and the lane is now used by quarry lorries to the Bestwood Colliery village.

I spent one summer weekend with Conservation and local volunteers, erecting the fencing to the left. There were a pair of willow warblers, whose brood of tiny newly hatched youngsters were huddled in a nest feet from the proceedings. As we worked with spades and shovel-holders the parent birds came by repeatedly with food clasped in their bills, sometimes within two or three feet of us.

Alexandra Lodge: Bestwood Country Park

The Collier's Path Route

By turning right at the top of the drive, you can walk the Collier's Path and still arrive at Alexandra Lodge. On a sunlit April day, with cock chaffinches singing, take in the beauty of the silver birch foliage clustered high against the flawless blue sky. In April and May you will hear, and hopefully glimpse, blackcap, garden-warblers and willow-warblers about the yew and rhododendron thickets. Several barely discernible streamlets will attract the birds down. Around the riding stables and paddocks, spotted flycatchers may be seen. Celandines star the glades and fenceside throughout April and May, when garlic mustard flowers by the fence posts.

Where the lanes divide, you need to turn left, through the fence gap with the sign *Bestwood Park Lodge* to your left. This is the Collier's Path. At your back between the riding stables and the field hedge, a lane leads in from Arnold. This is the route the colliers walked to and from the Bestwood Colliery.

There are pleasant undulating fields to your right, and the lure of the old or regenerated woodland glades ahead. Bramble and white dead nettle fringe the path. Gale-felled trees have been left to provide insect food for the birds.

The path dips near the gorse thickets. Some of the sycamores ahead are standing, but dead. Another bird species you may glimpse here is the tree pipit. From March to June, a dusk walk should reward you with sightings of 'roding' woodcock, as each male patrols his territorial boundary in flight.

This is good woodcock country — only a short distance from the Nottingham city centre! The fluting and 'ker-wick' calls of tawny owls may well serve as the only background sounds to these dusk forays.

You could see grey squirrel, jay and sparrowhawk if you are walking quietly in daylight and perhaps an unexpected visitor, like the merlin I flushed from the bracken fronds one September morning.

The Collier's Path continues down to Alexandra Lodge. Walking directly down from Alexandra Lodge takes you to the Bestwood Colliery village. Quarry lorries use the lane and you should walk facing the oncoming traffic.

As a homeward bound alternative you can, however, take the path just by the classroom on the left, bypassing the toilet block and children's play area then wend your way to the crown of the slope. Make the sandpath descent though birches and sycamores to the track which, if you turn right, will take you back to the winding house car park or the bus stop opposite the shop.

From this car park, if you are on foot and parked at Bulwell Hall, you need to retrace your route along the back path by Forge Farm, then cross Moor Road and turn left to Mill Close.

After walking this and having crossed the railway, the narrow track will take you into the Nottingham–Hucknall Road which you need to cross. Bear left just before the houses begin, to take the footpath to Bulwell Hall.

Alexandra Lodge To The Rectory Gateway

With Alexandra Lodge at your back and walking towards Bestwood Colliery village, you will see the expected sycamores and yew, particularly on the left, while horse chestnut trees form a dominating line to the right.

In April notice the ground ivy flowering above the beds of leaf litter. Opposite the Woodman's Cottage, forget-me-nots usually flower along the fence bottom. Rabbits can sometimes be glimpsed, and if you are walking quietly near daybreak or dusk, the occasional fox.

The last residence on the right before you reach the lorry route is the Old Rectory, with a splendid stand of Scots pine dominating the rear slope.

Alexandra Lodge

Designed as the formal north entrance to the Bestwood Lodge estate, Alexandra Lodge was completed as a two-family residence in 1876. The architect was Samuel Saunders Telon, who was a staunch admirer of church architecture. What you are looking at today is a Gothic style entrance, across which the lodgegates were positioned, and a half-timbered stage with a pyramidal shaped roof of double pitch.

Bestwood Lodge

Still an impressive building, Bestwood Lodge was built and completed to Telon's design in 1865. Sir Harold and Lady Bowden lived here for a time and the drive leading up from what is now Queen's Bower Road was lined with limes and oaks. The drive swept directly round into the main courtyard.

The banqueting bar of the current hotel, was once the conservatory, and the adjacent bar the orangery. The red plush upholstery is as impressive as the heavy wrought iron chandelier. During the last war the Army moved in and remained there for thirty-eight years, finally leaving in the autumn of 1977. Local residents remember the grounds being 'strewn throughout with tents and billet huts'.

Why So Many Sycamores?

While employed as a ranger at Bestwood, I was often asked this question. The reason why the self-regenerating and alarmingly prolific sycamore has taken hold in Big Wood is due to the fact that the fine mature timbers were taken out by contractors and used commercially just after the last war, long before this area became a country park.

Deer

Park, originally spelt as 'parke' is a Norman word denoting 'the place at which the deer are kept'. If you read Bestwood's history you will see that in the reign of Henry VIII, six hundred and ninety-one fallow deer and one hundred and fourteen red were kept at Bestwood.

In the mid 1970s a solitary black fallow buck caused some speculation as to whether it had strayed in from Annesley or the Rufford/Clipstone Forest area.

Nottinghamshire writers available from Five Leaves

Holiday by *Stanley Middleton*
0 907123 43 0, 240 pages, £7.99
A re-issue of the Booker Prize winning *Holiday*.
"As good as any novelist writing" **Daily Telegraph**

Stanley Middleton at Eighty
Edited by *David Belbin and John Lucas*
0 907123 38 4, 178 pages, £9.99
Includes essays by A.S. Byatt, Ronald Blythe and others, an in-depth interview with Stanley Middleton, together with three uncollected short stories and a lecture on old age by the Booker Prize winning author.

Haunting Time by *David Belbin*
0 907123 62 7, 195 pages, £4.99
Eerie stories for young adults.

Water by *Sue Thomas*
0 907123 51 1, 162 pages, £7.99
In the end she was forced to take her chances on the open ocean and there, off the coast of Scotland, she drowned him because she thought he deserved it. He probably did.
"...a dreamy novel, pulled along by a thread of emotion."
Los Angeles Times

City of Crime Edited by *David Belbin*
0 907123 12 0, 248 pages, £7.99
New crime short stories by Nottingham writers Catherine Arnold, David Belbin, Robert Cordell, Michael Eaton, Raymond Flynn, John Harvey, HRF Keating, Robert McMinn, Stanley Middleton, Peter Mortimer, Brendan Murphy, Julie Myerson, Frank Palmer, Alan Sillitoe and Keith Wright.

Mansfield Tales by *Keith Taylor*
0 907123 13 9, 46 pages, £3.99
A collection of ten short stories based on real events in Mansfield's eventful past.